D0297039

MARY ROSE'S
1001 COUNTRY COOKERY TIPS

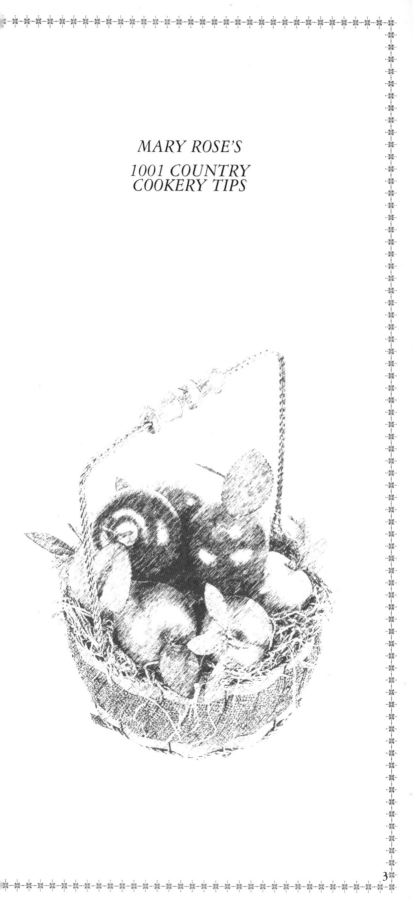

Published in the United Kingdom Exclusively for

SELECTABOOK
Folly Road
Roundway
Devizes
Wiltshire SN10 2HR

Produced by TAJ BOOKS
27 Ferndown Gardens
Cobham
Surrey
KT11 2BH
United Kingdom

Email : info@tajbooks.com

Text © 2002 Mary Rose Quigg
Design & Layout © 2002 TAJ BOOKS LTD

ISBN 1-84406-001-2

Printed and bound in China

ONTENTS

Acknowledgements

My thanks to Joe, Karen, Arleen, Orla, Cathal and Brenda for their encouragement and support. I am also indebted to family and friends who gave me recipes over the years.

$\mathcal{I}$NTRODUCTION

"When baking follow directions,
when cooking, go by your own taste"

"Cookery is not chemistry. It is an art.
It requires instinct and taste
rather than exact measurements"

In this book I have compiled a collection of my favourite recipes adapted over the years for use at home and at work. You will find throughout the book that ingredients for the dishes are generally available in local supermarkets or if you are into cooking then you will probably have many of them in your kitchen.

The recipes can be used for day to day cooking or for entertaining. Each section has a wide range to choose from with some useful hints included. You may notice that I use cream and butter frequently. Since we are all increasingly conscious of healthy eating, you can choose to use low fat alternatives but if you follow the saying "use everything in moderation" then used sparingly, butter and cream are usually best to enhance the flavour of many dishes.

I have shared many of these recipes with disenchanted cooks and teenagers and once they realised how simple it was to make a tasty pate, soup or casserole they discovered the pleasure of cooking. Some of them progressed to try baking or making preserves and found that there is nothing to beat a slice of home-made wheaten bread covered with blackcurrant jam!

I hope you enjoy making many of the dishes in this book and that they become firm favourites for years to come.

MARY ROSE

"Some people like to paint a picture, or do gardening or build a boat in the basement. Other people get a tremendous pleasure out of the kitchen, because cooking is just as creative and imaginative an activity as drawing, or woodcarving, or music"

JULIA CHILD

COOK'S TIPS

Serve melba toast with mousse appetisers. Toast slices of sandwich pan bread. Cut off the crusts. Using a thin bladed sharp knife split each slice of toast in half horizontally. Scrape off any small dough lumps. Bake, cut side up, in a hot oven or under a grill until golden, crisp and curled.

To ripen hard avocados, wrap in a paper bag with an orange, apple or banana and leave at room temperature.

To store half an avocado, leave the stone in it and smear lemon juice over the cut surface. Wrap tightly in cling-film until ready to use.

To stop discolouration of avocado mousse or dip, put the stones back into the mixture (temporarily) and smooth clingfilm right down on the surface to exclude any air - the browning is caused by oxidation.

Melons make a lovely appetiser, they can be served with slices of Parma Ham or smoked trout fillets.

If you are storing a melon in the refrigerator make sure to keep it in a sealed plastic bag or it will absorb the flavours of other food. Remove it from the refrigerator 30 minutes before serving to lose some of the chill.

To test melon for ripeness, press the opposite end of the fruit from the stalk with your thumb - if it `gives' a bit, then the fruit is ripe. It should also have a fragrant smell.

Asparagus should have the white skin removed from the lower end of the stalks, wash well and trim the stalks to an even length. Tie into a bundle and stand in a saucepan, tips upwards. Fill the saucepan with salted, boiling water up to below the tips. Cover the tips with tin foil so that the steam will cook them. cook for 10-15 minutes. Serve with hollandaise sauce or hot melted butter

Before slicing smoked salmon remove any bones with a pair of tweezers.

To serve smoked salmon - slice very thinly and serve with slices of lemon, a few capers, thinly sliced onion rings and buttered brown bread.

APPETISERS

MACKEREL PATE

8oz(225g) smoked mackerel
4oz(125g) cottage or cream cheese
2tsp horseradish sauce
1/2pt(150ml) natural yoghurt
1tbsp lemon juice
1tbsp tomato puree
salt and black pepper

Place all the ingredients in a bowl and mash well together.
Chill before serving with brown bread or toast fingers.
For a spicier flavour add a small finely chopped red onion and a drop or two of Tabasco.

SMOKED TROUT PATE

6oz(150g) cream cheese
12oz(300g) smoked trout fillets
2tsp creamed horseradish
juice and rind of lemon
salt and pepper

Cream the cheese until soft, flake the smoked trout and add to the cheese with the horseradish, lemon juice and rind. Season to taste. Spoon into 4 moulds or one large one, leave to chill. Smoked mackerel or salmon can also be used. Use cottage cheese with smoked mackerel and omit the horseradish with the smoked salmon.

SMOKED SALMON MOUSSE

1/2pt(300ml) milk
1 onion halved
1 carrot chopped
6 peppercorns
parsley
1/2oz(12g) butter, 1oz(25g) flour
1/8pt(75ml) chicken stock
1/2 oz(12g) gelatine, juice 1/2 lemon,
6oz(175g) smoked salmon, 2tbsp mayonnaise
1/4pt(150ml) cream, whipped

Add onion, carrot, parsley and peppercorns to milk, bring to the boil and infuse for 15 minutes. Strain and make white sauce with butter and flour. Cover with greaseproof paper and allow to cool. Dissolve gelatine in the hot stock. Allow to cool and fold into white sauce. Add chopped smoked salmon, mayonnaise and lemon juice. Whip cream and fold in. Pour into oiled mould and leave to set. Serves 4-6.

SMOKED & FRESH SALMON MOUSSE

12oz(350g) fresh salmon (no skin or bones)
little oil, salt and pepper
1tbsp lemon juice
3tbsp fish stock or white wine
1/2oz(12g) gelatine
1/2pt(300ml) yoghurt or cream
2tbsp thick mayonnaise
1tbsp tomato puree
4oz(125g) smoked salmon
2 egg whites

Place the fish into boiling water, add oil, seasoning, and half the lemon juice, poach gently for 8 minutes or until cooked. Drain and flake finely while still warm. Put 3tbsp fish stock or wine into a bowl over a pan of hot water and sprinkle gelatine on top, allow to dissolve. Cool slightly, add rest of lemon juice, yoghurt/cream, mayonnaise and tomato puree. Fold in the flaked salmon, allow the mixture to chill until it begins to stiffen slightly. Finely chop smoked salmon, whisk egg whites until stiff and fold both into the mixture. Spoon into an oiled mould and allow to set. Turn out on a bed of lettuce and garnish with cucumber and lemon slices. Serves

SMOKED FISH TRIO

8oz(225g) smoked trout fillet, skinned
8oz(225g) smoked mackerel fillet, skinned
8oz(225g) smoked salmon trimmings
8oz(225g) unsalted butter, melted
6tbsp double cream
4tbsp lemon juice
1tsp creamed horseradish, 1tbsp cottage cheese
freshly ground white pepper
Cayenne pepper, 1/2tsp dill

Rub a little oil over a 1lb(450g)loaf tin and line with cling film. Flake the trout and place in a food processor, or mash, with one third of the melted butter (about 6tbsp), 2tbsp cream, 1tbsp lemon juice, horseradish and white pepper to taste. Spoon into the prepared tin and level the surface.Process the flaked mackerel with half the remaining butter, 1tbsp lemon juice, 1tbsp cream, cottage cheese and white pepper to taste. Spread evenly over the trout pate.Process the smoked salmon with the remaining butter, 3tbsp cream, 2tbsp lemon juice, dill, white and cayenne pepper to taste. Layer on top of mackerel mixture. Cover with cling film and leave in the refrigerator for at least 3 hours. Turn out onto a plate and cut into slices. These slices can be individually wrapped in cling film and frozen for up to 1 month. Defrost as required, in the refrigerator. Makes 8-10 slices.

SALMON LOAF

1tbsp vegetable oil,
8oz(225g) cooked salmon,
3 hard-boiled eggs, 6oz(175g) tomatoes
4 pickled gherkins, chopped
1-2tbsp chopped parsley, salt and black pepper
6-8fl oz(200ml) mayonnaise,
2tbsp creamy milk,
1/2tbsp lemon juice
1oz(25g) gelatine dissolved in 1tbsp hot water,

Grease a 2lb loaf tin or ring mould. Combine the flaked salmon, chopped eggs, tomatoes, gherkins, parsley, salt and pepper. In a separate bowl combine the mayonnaise, milk, lemon juice, and melted gelatine. Stir into the salmon mixture and put into tin. Chill for at least 2 hours. To remove run a knife around the edge and dip the base in hot water. Serve on a bed of lettuce and chopped cucumber. The ingredients can be altered according to what is available e.g. tinned salmon can be used instead of fresh. Serves 6

MARINATED SALMON

2tbsp sea salt, 2tbsp caster sugar
2tsp crushed ground black pepper
4tbsp chopped dill, 8tbsp lime juice
3-4lb salmon fillets with skin intact

Mix all the ingredients except salmon. Spoon a quarter of the mixture over the base of an non-metallic dish. Lay on salmon fillet, skin side down. Spoon over half the mixture, cover with second fillet, skin side up. Cover with remaining mixture. Cover with greaseproof paper, weigh down with a 2lb(900g) weight for two days, turn occasionally. Serve thinly sliced with lemon wedges and brown bread.
Serves 8-10.

SALMON & CHEESE TOASTIES

2oz(50g) smoked salmon. thinly sliced
8 thick slices of French roll, buttered
4oz(125g) cheese, Lemon wedges

Oven 400°F/200°C/Gas 6.
Place slices of smoked salmon on top of buttered bread, cover with cheese. Grill or bake for 4-5 minutes until cheese melts. Serve hot garnished with lemon.
* *For a snack use a French stick instead of bread, and a little Worcestershire sauce over the cheese*

AVOCADO & PRAWN MOUSSE

1tbsp gelatine
1/4pt (150ml) white wine
2 large ripe avocados
1/4pt (150ml) mayonnaise
grated zest 1/2 lemon, salt and pepper
1/4pt (150ml) double cream, whipped
6oz(100g) peeled prawns, chopped
parsley sprigs

Dissolve the gelatine in the white wine. Peel halve and stone avocados. Chop the flesh roughly and place in a blender with the mayonnaise, gelatine, lemon zest and seasoning. Liquidise until smooth. Pour into a bowl and allow to stand until almost setting, fold in the whipped cream and shellfish. Divide the mixture between 6 dishes and chill until set. Decorate with some peeled prawns and parsley.

PRAWN & MUSHROOM VOL-AU-VENTS

1 large onion, 8oz(225g) mushrooms
1oz(25g) butter, 1tbsp oil
1tbsp brandy,   1tbsp white wine, 1/4pt(150ml) cream
salt and black pepper, pinch curry powder
8oz(225g) prawns
8 medium vol-au-vent cases (or 4 large cases)

Peel and finely chop onion, slice mushrooms. Melt the butter and oil in a saucepan and fry onion until soft. Add the mushrooms, raise the heat and stirring well, quickly cook the mushrooms until soft. Add the wine and brandy, stir over high heat until most of the liquid has evaporated. Add the cream, bring to the boil and simmer until thick. Add curry powder and season to taste. Stir in the prawns and heat through. Heat vol-au-vent cases for a few minutes in a hot oven, fill with the prawn mixture. Serve immediately.

PRAWN COCKTAIL

2tbsp mayonnaise or salad cream
1tbsp whipped cream, 1tsp lemon juice
1tbsp tomato sauce, few drops tabasco
finely chopped cucumber
Cooked prawns,   lettuce and tomatoes

Mix first six ingredients together to make the sauce. Shred the lettuce, chop tomatoes and place some of each in the bottom of 4 glass dishes. Fill the glasses with cooked prawns and pour the sauce over them. Decorate with a shake of paprika and a slice of lemon.

CRAB & AVOCADO WITH YOGHURT DRESSING

6oz(175g) crab meat
2tbsp mayonnaise
few drops tabasco
1-2tbsp chopped chives
1 clove garlic, crushed
salt and freshly ground black pepper
3 large ripe avocado
lemon juice

DRESSING

1/4pt(150ml) natural yoghurt
2tbsp mayonnaise
1 clove garlic, crushed
2tbsp each chives and parsley, chopped

For dressing, beat all the ingredients together and season to taste.Combine the crab meat, mayonnaise, tabasco, chives, garlic and seasoning. Leave for half an hour for the flavours to mingle. Just before serving peel the skin from the avocados, half lengthways and remove the stones. Rub over with lemon juice to prevent discolouration. Cut a slice from the rounded side of four halves so that it will sit evenly on the plate. Fill the cavities with crab mixture. Slice the remaining avocado and place on top of the crab. Serve with dressing.

CRAB & MUSHROOM RAMEKINS

4oz(125g) small button mushrooms
1oz(25g) butter, salt and pepper
4oz(125g) crab meat
1/2pt(300ml) cheese sauce, 1oz(25g) cheese
parsley and paprika

Oven 400°C200°F/Gas 6
Cook mushrooms in butter until tender, save 4 for garnish, place the rest of the mushrooms in ramekin dishes. Season lightly and top with crab meat, then sauce. Grate cheese over, and bake for 10-15 minutes Top with mushroom, parsley and a dusting of paprika.

CRAB MEAT SHELLS

2 oranges and 1 grapefruit, peeled and segmented
4oz(125g) Edam cheese, diced, 1/4 cucumber chopped
6oz(175g) crab meat, 1tbsp mayonnaise
parsley

Reserve two orange segments for garnish, chop the rest with grapefruit. Mix with cheese and cucumber. Mix crab meat with mayonnaise, Place crab meat mixture on one half of each of 4 scallop shells or small plates, and fruit mixture on other half. Garnish with orange and parsley.

MOULES MARINIÈRE

12-15 mussels per person
1 onion, finely chopped, 1oz(25g) butter, 1tbsp oil
1/4pt(150ml) dry white wine
1tbsp finely chopped parsley, bay leaf, thyme
freshly ground black pepper
1/4pt(150ml) fresh cream

Check that the mussels shells are closed tightly or close when lightly tapped. Discard any that don't close or are broken. Steep them in lightly salted water with a little oatmeal added for a few hours to remove the sand and grit. Scrub the mussels and remove the `beard'. Rinse and dry with a tea towel before adding to the saucepan. Saute onion in the melted butter and oil for a few minutes until soft, add the remaining ingredients and simmer for a few minutes before adding the dried mussels. Cover and cook over a high heat for a few minutes until shells open, shake the saucepan occasionally. Remove from the heat and take the top shell from the mussels and arrange in a heated dish, keep warm. Return the pan to the heat and reduce the liquor by half, add about 1/4pt fresh cream. Pour sauce over the mussels and serve with a sprinkling of chopped parsley. Sauce for 4 - 6.

GARLIC CRUMBED MUSSELS

10-12 cooked mussels per person
3oz(75g) butter, 2 cloves garlic, crushed, juice half a lemon
freshly ground black pepper, 1tbsp freshly chopped parsley
Fresh white breadcrumbs

Place the mussels in an ovenproof dish. Melt butter, add garlic and heat, add lemon juice, pepper and parsley. Pour over the mussels and then shake a little breadcrumbs over each mussel. Either cook under a hot grill or in a hot oven for a few minutes and serve hot.

SCALLOPS IN CREAM SAUCE

4fl oz(120ml) white wine, 1/2tsp lemon juice
1lb(450g) scallops
1tbsp butter, 2tbsp flour
1/4pt (150ml) single cream
1/4tsp salt, 1/4tsp pepper,
1/8tsp cayenne pepper
1oz(25g) Gruyere cheese, grated

In a heavy-based saucepan, bring wine and lemon juice to the boil, reduce heat and add the scallops. Simmer gently for 8 -10 minutes. Remove the pan from heat and cool. Strain the liquid. Slice the scallops in half. Melt butter, add flour and cooking liquid and make a smooth sauce. Cook for 3 minutes. Stir in cream and seasoning, cook a further 2 minutes. Fold the scallops into the sauce. Spoon onto 4 flat dishes, sprinkle cheese on top and brown under grill for a few minutes.

TUNA & ORANGE COCKTAIL

lettuce, washed and shredded
8oz(225g) can tuna fish in brine
3 mandarin oranges, peeled and segmented
3tbsp salad cream, 1tbsp Worcestershire sauce
1tbsp tomato puree, 2tbsp milk, 1tbsp lemon juice
salt and black pepper

Place a bed of lettuce on 4 individual dishes. Reserve a few mandarin segments for garnish. Chop the remainder and mix with flaked tuna fish. Combine the remaining ingredients together and stir into the fish mixture. Spoon mixture onto the lettuce and garnish with orange.

CARIBBEAN COCKTAIL

2 grapefruit
4oz(125g) cooked chicken, diced
2 sticks celery, finely chopped
1 small can pineapple pieces, drained
3tbsp mayonnaise,   salt and pepper, 5tbsp mango chutney
4 glace cherries

Halve grapefruit and remove pulp, discard pith and pips and chop flesh. Combine with rest of ingredients. Divide between shells and decorate with cherries. Serve chilled.

CHICKEN TERRINE

11/2lb(700g) chicken breast, cut into chunks
3 eggs size 3, juice half a lemon
2tbsp fresh tarragon, 2tbsp fresh parsley, pinch salt
1/2pt(300ml) double cream
2tbsp green peppercorns
cooked whole green beans and whole small carrots

Oven to 300°F/180°C/Gas4.
Put a roasting tin half-filled with water (a bain-marie) in the oven to heat. Line a 2lb loaf tin with parchment. Process the first seven ingredients to a puree. Stir in peppercorns. Place one-third of the chicken mixture in the base of the tin and level. Cover with a layer of beans. Cover with one-third of mixture and level. Place a layer of carrot on top and cover with remaining mixture. Place the loaf tin in the bain-marie and cook for 40-45 minutes. Tip onto a plate remove the parchment. Serve in slices with a tomato sauce. Serves 4-6.

MUSHROOMS IN MUSTARD MAYONNAISE

12oz(350g) button mushrooms
1tbsp brandy
3tbsp water, squeeze lemon juice
seasoning
2tbsp mayonnaise
1tbsp mild French mustard

Quarter large mushrooms, or use small mushrooms whole. Put into a pan with brandy, water, lemon juice and a shake of salt. Toss over a good heat until cooked but still crisp. Drain well reserving liquor. Reduce the liquor to one tablespoon. Pour into a small dish. Make dressing by blending the mayonnaise, mustard and liquor. Stir in the mushrooms and chill well. For garlic mayonnaise, add 1 crushed garlic clove and 1tbsp tomato puree to 1/4pt(150ml) mayonnaise and mix well. Spoon into a serving bowl and sprinkle with paprika.

CURRIED EGGS

9 hard boiled eggs
1tbsp curried fruit chutney, 1tsp curry paste
2tsp mayonnaise
1tsp horseradish sauce, seasoning

Halve the eggs, remove the yolks, place in a bowl, add the white of one egg, mash well. Add the remaining ingredients, mix well. Spoon back into the egg whites, put a raisin from the chutney on top.

POTTED DUCK WITH ORANGE

4-6oz(125g-175g) roast duck (or any left-over meat)
3oz(75g) butter, 1 small onion, finely chopped
grated rind of one small orange
1-2tbsp freshly chopped parsley, salt and pepper

Finely mince the cooked meat in a food processor or mincer.
Melt half the butter in a saucepan, add the onion and cook
until soft. Add the meat, orange rind, chopped parsley and
seasoning to taste. Mix well. Melt the remaining butter, allow to
cool slightly and skim off the white froth. Pour the clarified
butter over the meat and allow to chill. Garnish with sprigs of
parsley or strips of orange rind. Serve with hot toast.

ASPARAGUS TARTS

8oz(225g) asparagus tips
1/4pt(150ml) single cream, 1/4pt(150ml) milk
3 eggs, 1/2tsp grated nutmeg
1/2oz(12g) unsalted butter, 8oz(225g) shortcrust pastry

Oven 275°F/140°C/Gas1.
Line six 3" tartlet tins with thinly rolled pastry. Bake blind for
15 minutes. Beat eggs with seasoning. Bring cream and milk to
the boil, pour over eggs, whisking well. Meanwhile cook
asparagus with tips out of water. Cut the tip of the asparagus
and chop the remainder into the cream mixture, add nutmeg,
blend together. Strain to remove strings. fill the tartlets and
add asparagus tips to each. Bake for 25 minutes. Serve hot with
a blob of unsalted butter on top. Serves 6.

SPEEDY LIVER PATE

8oz(225g) lamb's liver, sliced thinly
2 fatty bacon rashers, de-rinded and chopped
1 medium onion, 1 garlic clove, chopped
4oz(125g) butter, 4-5tbsp cream
2tbsp chopped parsley, salt and pepper

Heat the butter in pan, add bacon and onion and cook gently
for 4-5 minutes. Add liver and cook a further 4 minutes, do not
over-cook. Put the pan contents into a food processor. Add
cream to the pan to absorb the meat juices. Add to the
processor with seasoning. Process until smooth. Place in a
mould, chill and serve with toast or brown bread.

COOK'S TIPS

When cooking meat bones or a chicken carcass for stock always keep at a gentle simmer as fast boiling will make the stock cloudy.

A certain amount of scum will rise to the surface when cooking stock. Skim away frequently by sliding a large spoon horizontally across the surface, gently lift off the scum and discard.

To remove fat from stock, allow to cool for 30 minutes, then skim off as above. To de-grease more thoroughly, leave to cool overnight and remove the solidified fat in the morning.

Avoid using turnips for soups, stew or stocks, etc, which you are not using the same day. Turnips go `off' more quickly than other vegetables.

A crustless slice of bread or a boiled potato put in the blender with a thin soup will make it velvety.

Always season soups or stews towards the end of cooking, when the liquid has been reduced. Do not add salt to pulses or beans at the beginning of cooking or it will make the skins split and harden the pulp.

Add 1tbsp prune juice to soups to enrich their flavour and colour. A lump of sugar added to clear soup will improve its appearance.

Don't waste leftover wine - pour it into an ice-cube tray and freeze. When making a soup or stew, add the cubes for improved flavour.

Add a raw potato to over salted soup and simmer for ten minutes. Remember to remove the potato before serving.

To avoid pea soup turning into pease pudding, add roux or cornflour to stabilise the proteins and keep the liquid at the required consistency.

Add some of the papery, outer, onion skin to a soup liquid to give it a lovely golden colour

For extra crunchy croutons, bake in the oven instead of frying. Cut thickly sliced bread into large cubes and place on a baking sheet, drizzle with a little oil and a sprinkling of Parmesan cheese, if liked. Bake at 350°F/180°C/Gas 4 for 10-15 minutes, turning regularly. Serve with soups or tossed in salads.

$\mathcal{S}$OUPS

ARTICHOKE SOUP

1 1/2lb(700g) artichokes or 2 tins artichokes
1/4 pt(150ml) milk, 2 rashers bacon
2 onions, 1 clove garlic, chopped
1oz(25g) butter, 2 small potatoes, sliced
1pt(600ml) chicken stock, 1/4pt(150ml) cider
seasoning, 1/4pt(150ml) cream

Scrub artichokes well and parboil in water. Pull off skins and finish cooking in milk with bacon. Sweat onions and garlic in butter. Add sliced potato, stock and cider. Bring to the boil and cook for 30 minutes. Add artichokes, milk and bacon (or tinned artichokes). Liquidise. Reheat with cream. Season to taste. Add a little chopped chervil. Serves 6

* For a chunkier soup — after cooking retain 1 artichoke and 1 rasher of bacon. Liquidise the rest. Roughly chop the reserved artichoke and bacon and return to soup

CREAM OF ASPARAGUS SOUP

1lb Asparagus or 2 tins whole asparagus spears
1oz(25g) butter, 1tbsp oil
1 onion, peeled and chopped
1 stick celery, sliced (optional)
1pt(600ml) chicken stock, 3tbsp white wine, juice 1 lemon
1/4pt(150ml) cream, salt and paprika pepper

Cut the heads off the asparagus and simmer them for a few minutes in lightly salted boiling water. Drain and refresh under cold running water. Reserve. Scrape the stalks, saute with the onion and celery in oil and butter. Add stock, wine and lemon juice, bring to the boil and simmer for 20 minutes. (if using canned asparagus - drain the asparagus and reserve half the liquid. Cut off the tips and keep to one side. chop the stalks and place them in a pan with the onion, celery, stock, wine, asparagus liquid and lemon juice.) Cool slightly and blend in a liquidiser to form a smooth puree or rub through a fine sieve. Season with salt and pepper. Stir in the asparagus tips and cream before serving. Heat through but do not boil. Can be served chilled. Serves 6

* After liquidising add 4oz frozen peas to the soup. Make sure they have defrosted before adding cream and asparagus tips

Broccoli & Apple Soup

1oz(25g) butter, 1tbsp oil
8oz Brambley apple, peeled, cored and chopped
1 onion, peeled and chopped
1lb(450g) fresh or frozen broccoli, chopped
1pt(600ml) vegetable stock
2tbsp white wine, 1tsp honey
salt and freshly ground black pepper
1/4pt(150ml) fresh cream

Melt the butter and oil and sauté, cook the onion and apple until softened but not coloured. Add the broccoli, stock and wine. Season with salt and pepper, cover, bring to the boil and simmer for 20 minutes. Cool slightly, liquidise until pureed. Stir in cream. Taste for seasoning. This soup can be served hot or chilled. Serves 6.
* Instead of broccoli use either cauliflower or Brussels sprouts

Lettuce Soup

1-2 heads of lettuce, 1 onion, 1 potato diced,
1oz(25g) butter, 1pt(600ml) milk
salt and pepper
1/2pt(300ml) chicken stock, 2tbsp white wine
4tbsp cream

Melt butter in pan. Shred lettuce and add to the pan with onion and potato. Fry gently, without browning, for five minutes. Add milk, stock and wine, bring to the boil, stirring continuously. Cover and simmer for 10-15 minutes. Rub through a sieve or liquidise and return to the pan. Season and reheat. Serve with a dollop of cream. Serves 6.

Carrot & Orange Soup

12oz(350g) carrots peeled and sliced
Juice of two large oranges
(reserve thinly pared rind of 1 orange)
2 medium sized onions peeled, chopped
4tbsp cream
1oz(25g) butter plus a little oil, salt and black pepper
11/2pt(900ml) chicken or vegetable stock
3tbsp white wine

Melt the butter and oil and stir in carrot and onion. Cover and allow the vegetables to cook gently for 5 minutes. Pour in stock and wine, bring to the boil, reduce heat and simmer for 15 minutes. Allow to cool slightly, liquidise or put through a sieve. Add orange juice and blend well. Return to the saucepan. Season to taste and reheat gently without boiling. Cut the orange rinds into fine strips and simmer in water for 5 minutes. Drain well and float on top of soup with a dollop of cream before serving. Serves 6.

LEEK & POTATO SOUP

1 large leek, chopped
12oz(350g) potatoes, diced
1oz(25g) butter, 1tbsp oil
2pt(1200ml) chicken stock
1/2pt(300ml) milk
parsley(optional)

Heat butter and oil in a pan. Add leeks and potato. Cover and cook gently for six minutes. Add chicken stock. Bring to the boil and gently simmer for half an hour until leeks are cooked. Cool and put through a sieve or liquidise. Return to pan and reheat before serving. Serves 6-8.

* This soup is best made several hours before serving to allow the mixture to become less glutinous

CHICKEN & POTATO SOUP

1oz(25g)butter, 1tbsp oil
1 onion, chopped
1-2 cloves garlic, crushed
2 boneless breasts of chicken
4oz(100g) mushrooms, chopped
1lb(450g) potatoes, diced, 2 sticks celery, finely diced
11/4pt(750ml) water plus 2 chicken stock cubes
1pt(600ml) milk
1/2tsp mixed herbs, freshly ground black pepper

Heat the oil and butter and saute the onion and garlic until soft but not brown. Cut the chicken into small pieces and add to the pan, cook until lightly golden. Add the mushrooms and fry until soft. Add the potatoes, celery, water and stock cubes, bring to the boil. Add milk, herbs and pepper. Bring to the boil and simmer for 20-25 minutes. Serves 6.

* To make an even more filling soup omit the mushrooms and instead add a can of haricot beans to the potatoes etc

MUSHROOM SOUP

1pt(600ml) chicken stock
2 onions, chopped, 1lb(450g) mushrooms, chopped
butter & oil, 2tsp marjoram
1 clove garlic, crushed, seasoning
3tbsp white wine
1/4pt(150ml) cream, 1oz(25g) rice

Sweat onions and garlic in melted butter and oil, sprinkle on marjoram, add half mushrooms and cook a few minutes. Add stock, seasoning, rice, and wine. Simmer for 30 minutes. Liquidise. Saute the remaining mushrooms, add to the soup and simmer for a few minutes. Add cream.

MINESTRONE SOUP

1 leek, 1 large onion
1 carrot, 2 stalks celery
6oz(175g) white or green cabbage
1 small pkt. frozen green beans
14oz(400g) can tomatoes
2tbsp chopped parsley, 1tsp basil
1tsp salt, black pepper
1tsp sugar
1 1/2pt(900ml) water
2oz(50g) broken macaroni
3oz(75g) grated cheese

Trim leek and clean thoroughly. Shred finely. Slice onion, carrot, celery and cabbage. Put prepared vegetables into a large pan, add green beans, tomatoes, herbs, seasoning and water. Bring to the boil, lower heat, cover, simmer for 1 hour. Add macaroni, simmer a further 15 minutes. Serve in warm bowls with cheese sprinkled on top. Serves 6.

* *Any of the small pasta shapes are suitable for minestrone simply adjust the cooking time accordingly*

MULLIGATAWNY SOUP
(CURRY SOUP)

1tbsp hot curry powder, 1tbsp tomato puree
1 small onion, chopped,
1 small cooking apple, cored and diced
1/2 cup rice, 1/2pt(300ml) chicken stock
1tbsp lime juice or pineapple juice, dash white wine
cream (optional), seasoning

Fry onion, stir in curry powder, puree and rice. Add stock and allow to boil. Add apple. When rice is cooked, liquidise the soup. Return to the pan and add lime or pineapple juice. If mixture is too thick add a little more stock. Add cream before serving. Serves 4

* *Vary the flavour with different kinds of curry paste. For example a Korma will give a mild flavour while a Vindaloo will be very hot*

FRENCH ONION SOUP

1oz(25g) butter, 1tbsp oil, 1lb(450g) onions, thinly sliced
2pt(1200ml) beef stock,
salt and black pepper, 3tbsp sherry or wine

Fry the onion in oil and butter until soft. Pour in stock and season to taste. Bring to the boil and simmer for 30 minutes. Add sherry or wine if used. Serve with cheese and crusty bread or garlic bread. Serves 6-8.

PEA & HAM SOUP

1oz(25g) butter, 1tbsp oil
1 onion, peeled, chopped, 1 clove garlic, crushed
12oz(350g) potatoes, peeled, cubed
2 sticks celery, sliced, 1lb(450g) green peas
11/2pt(900ml) vegetable or chicken stock
2tbsp white wine, 2tbsp fresh cream
6oz(175g) cooked ham, cubed
parsley sprigs to garnish

Melt the butter with oil in a large pan. Add the onion and garlic, fry gently until softened but not brown. Add potatoes and celery, cook for five minutes. Add peas, stock and wine. Season with salt and pepper, bring to the boil, simmer for 30 minutes. Remove from the heat, allow to cool. Liquidise until smooth. Stir in cream and ham, heat until hot, but not boiling. Taste for seasoning. Garnish with parsley. Serves 6.
* For an extra lavish soup fry 4 rashers of bacon. Chop into pieces and scatter over each bowl of soup

CREAM OF
ROAST VEGETABLE SOUP

2oz(50g) butter, 1tbsp oil
few rosemary needles, snipped into small pieces
2 red peppers, halved and de-seeded
2 green peppers, halved and de-seeded
2 small courgettes, cut into thick slices
2 large flat mushrooms, peeled and quartered
1 onion, peeled and quartered,
1 clove garlic, peeled, salt and black pepper
2oz(50g) red split lentils, rinsed
11/2pt(900ml) vegetable or chicken stock
1/4pt(125ml) cream

Oven to 375°F/190°C/Gas5.
Mix melted butter, oil and rosemary together in a large bowl. Toss the prepared vegetables in this mixture and then arrange them on a roasting tin. Season with salt and pepper. Place the tin in the oven and roast uncovered for 20 minutes. Put the lentils and stock in a large saucepan, bring to the boil and simmer for 10 minutes. Remove the roasted vegetables from the oven. Place the peppers in a plastic bag and tie loosely. When cool enough to handle, remove the skin and discard. Add all the vegetables to the stock mixture, bring to the boil and simmer for 20 minutes. Allow to cool slightly before liquidising. Return to the pan and stir in cream, taste for seasoning. Reheat gently but do not boil. Serves 6-8.

RED PEPPER SOUP

1oz(25g) butter, 1tbsp oil
1 red/white onion, chopped, 1 clove garlic, crushed
11/2pt (900ml)chicken stock, 2tbsp sherry
3 red peppers, de-seeded and finely diced
8oz(227g) chopped, tinned tomatoes, 1tsp sugar
1tsp fresh parsley, chopped
1oz(25g) plain flour, 1oz(25g) butter
1tsp fresh chives, chopped

Melt the butter and oil, add the onion and garlic, saute until soft but not brown. Add the stock, sherry, peppers, tomatoes, sugar and parsley. Cover and simmer for 20-25 minutes. Stir flour into the melted butter, add to the soup whisking until it boils, simmer for five minutes.Garnish with chives. For a smooth soup, liquidise and strain. Serves 6.

* To make the soup hotter add a few drops of Tabasco sauce

TOMATO, APPLE
& CELERY CREAM SOUP

1pt(600ml) chicken stock
4oz(125g) onions, finely chopped
5-6oz(175g) tomatoes, 5-6oz(175g) apples, sliced
5-6oz(175g) celery cut into 2" lengths
2oz(50g) butter, 2fl oz(60ml) dry sherry
1/4tsp salt, black pepper
pinch grated nutmeg and ground ginger
apple slices and snipped fresh chives to garnish

Melt the butter, add onion and cook gently until golden. Add sherry, vegetables, fruit, spices and seasoning. Place a double thickness of greaseproof paper, dampened with cold water, over the ingredients and cover the pan with a lid. Simmer for 1 hour, stir regularly. Add the stock and stir well. Liquidise and press through a sieve. Return to a clean pan. Reheat, check seasoning. Garnish with apple and chives. Serves 4-6.

RICH TOMATO SOUP

1oz(25g) butter, 1tbsp oil
4 rashers streaky bacon, de-rinded and chopped
1 onion, chopped, 1 clove garlic, crushed
2 sticks celery, sliced,
1tbsp brown sugar
1/2pt(900ml) chicken stock, 3tbsp red wine
2lb(1kg) ripe tomatoes or 2 tins chopped tomatoes
salt and freshly ground black pepper
4tbsp freshly chopped parsley, 2tbsp tomato puree
1oz(25g) flour, 1oz(25g) butter
lightly whipped cream

Heat the oil and butter, saute the onions, garlic, bacon and celery until soft but not brown. Add stock, wine, sugar, tomatoes, tomato puree, seasoning and parsley. Cover and bring to the boil, simmer for 30 minutes. Blend in a liquidiser and then sieve to remove seeds. Make roux from butter and flour and add to soup whisking well to thicken. Serve with swirls of cream and sprinkle with chopped parsley. Serves 6-8.

* *Plain fromage frais or yogurt work as well as cream and are less fattening*

PRAWN CHOWDER

2oz(50g) butter
3 stalks celery, 1 onion, 1/2 green pepper
1/2pt(300ml) chicken stock, 8oz(225g) tin tomatoes
1 bay leaf, salt, pepper, paprika
8oz(225g) peeled prawns, 1 small pkt frozen peas

Melt the butter in a pan, add the finely chopped celery, onion and pepper, cook until onion is transparent. Add the stock, tomatoes and bay leaf, season and simmer for 20 minutes. Add prawns and peas, stir well. Cook a further 10 minutes. Serves 4.

* *To make a more substantial chowder — add a small can of corn before cooking*

CHUNKY FISH SOUP

1oz(25g) butter, 1tbsp oil
2 leeks, sliced, 2 sticks celery, chopped
14oz(395g) can chopped tomatoes
8 mussels, canned or fresh
2 small squid, cleaned and cut into rings(optional)
1lb(450g) mixed fish (cod, haddock, whiting)
1tsp turmeric, 1/2pt(300ml) white wine
1/2pt(300ml) fish/vegetable stock
chopped parsley to garnish,
croutons and grated Parmesan cheese to serve

Heat the butter/oil in a large pan, add leeks and celery and cook for 5 minutes until soft. Add turmeric, tomatoes, wine and stock, Bring to the boil and simmer gently for 15 minutes. Fillet the fish and cut in chunks. Add fish, mussels and squid (if using). Simmer a further 5-8 minutes. Serve hot garnished with parsley, croutons and grated Parmesan cheese. Serves 4-6. To prepare squid, remove head and tentacles by pulling gently. The inedible head and ink sac will come away together. Feel around the body pouch for the plasticky quill-shaped backbone, remove and discard. Slip a finger under membrane covering body pouch and peel away gently.

WHEN BUYING FISH

When choosing whole fish look for - bright, shiny, prominent eyes, bright red coloured gills, skin, smooth to touch with a sheen, clean, fresh seaweed smell, no fishy smell.

When purchasing fillets of fish look for - clean fresh smell, flesh should be translucent rather than milky white in colour, the flesh should be close textured, no reddening along the backbone, preferably fish should be displayed on a bed of ice.

Always eat fish when fresh, preferably the day of purchase, but it can be kept up to 24 hours in the refrigerator, if it is loosely wrapped in foil.

Fish can be classified in three groups:
White Fish - Sometimes called lean fish as all the oils are contained in the liver and this is removed during gutting. Some of the fish that fall into this category are - cod, haddock, whiting, place and sole
Oily Fish - As the title suggests these fish have the oils distributed throughout the flesh - salmon, mackerel, herring and trout.
Shellfish - These are divided into two areas - crustaceans (lobster, crab, prawns) and molluscs (mussels, oysters, scallops and whelks.

FISH STOCK

To 2lb(900g) of sole turbot or bass bones add:
1 small onion, 1 carrot, 1 celery stick
2oz(50g) mushroom stalks and peelings
1 sprig parsley, 1 bay leaf
juice of 1/2 a lemon
1/2 bottle dry white wine, 2pt(1200ml) cold water
salt, 6 white peppercorns

Wash the bones well in cold water. Put all the ingredients except salt into a pan and simmer for 20 minutes only. Strain, add salt to taste, and cool ready for use.

ISH

COD CASSEROLE

4 cod steaks
1 onion, 1/2 green pepper, chopped finely
3 ripe tomatoes, skinned and sliced
2tbsp peeled, chopped cucumber
1/2oz(12g) butter
1/2pt(150ml) sour cream
1/2tsp paprika pepper, salt and pepper

Oven 350°F/180°C/Gas4.
Sprinkle cucumber with salt and leave to drain in a colander for
20 minutes. Dry well. Butter a baking dish, cover the bottom
with a layer of chopped onion, pepper and cucumber. Arrange
the sliced tomatoes on this layer and the cod steaks on top.
Season. Combine the cream and paprika and pour over the fish.
Cover tightly and bake for 25 minutes.

OCEAN ROLLS

4 white fish fillets
1tbsp lemon juice
1tbsp butter, 1 shallot, finely chopped
4oz(125g) frozen prawns, thawed, 4oz(125g) crab meat
4tbsp sweetcorn, cooked
1tbsp cornflour, mixed with 1tbsp white wine
1/2tsp dried dill, 1/2tsp salt, 1/2tsp black pepper
4tbsp double cream
12fl oz(360ml) dry white wine
1 bay leaf, 1 small onion

Sprinkle fillets with lemon juice. Melt butter and fry shallot for
3-4 minutes. Stir in prawns, crab meat, sweetcorn, seasoning
and cream. Cook stirring constantly for 3 minutes. Remove pan
from the heat, spoon equal amounts of mixture over each fillet.
Roll up fillets and secure with thread. In a pan bring wine, bay
leaf and onion to boil. Lower the fish fillets into the liquid in
one layer. Reduce the heat and simmer for 5 minutes. Turn the
fish rolls over and simmer a further 8 minutes. Lift the rolls
onto a heated serving plate, keep warm. Remove the bay leaves
and onion from the liquid. Bring the liquid to the boil and
reduce to one-third. Reduce heat and add cornflour, simmer for
5 minutes. Serve sauce with fish, duchesse potatoes and peas

** Vary the sauce by adding chopped parsley or chopped capers. Alternatively,
omit the cornflour and instead stir 1/2pt thick cream into the cooled liquid.
Season to taste*

MONKFISH WITH GARLIC & HERB BUTTER

11/2lb(700g) filleted monkfish tail
3oz(75g) butter, 1tbsp freshly chopped herbs
2 cloves garlic, crushed
seasoned flour, 1 egg, beaten
3oz(75g) fresh white breadcrumbs
juice of half a lemon

Oven 375°F/190°C/Gas5.
Soften butter and add herbs and garlic, chill. Make a slit in each monkfish fillet and pack with the chilled butter. Fold up to enclose the butter. Toss each fillet in seasoned flour, dip in egg and breadcrumbs, press the crumbs firmly onto the fish. Place in a buttered, ovenproof dish, dribble a little melted butter over and sprinkle with lemon juice. Cook for 15-20 minutes or until fish is cooked (time depends on the thickness of the fillet).

PLAICE WITH CARROT SAUCE

8 plaice fillets
1 bay leaf, 3 sprigs coriander

SAUCE

1/2pt(300ml) fish stock
6oz(175g) carrots, peeled, juice of 1/2 orange
3tbsp natural yoghurt, 1tbsp cornflour
3fl oz(90ml) single cream
lemon slices, fresh coriander, salt and black pepper

Oven 375°F/190°C/Gas 5.
Wash and skin plaice fillets. Roll up neatly. Place in a greased oven- proof dish with bay leaf, 1 sprig coriander and 3tbsp of fish stock. Cover tightly and bake for 15 minutes. Place the carrots, orange juice, 2 sprigs of coriander and remaining fish stock into a pan. Cover and simmer for 20 minutes. Cool slightly, liquidise and strain. Mix yoghurt and cornflour, stir into the sauce with cream. Reheat gently but do not boil. Place the fish on a preheated plate, garnish with lemon and coriander. Serve with sauce.

STUFFED WHITING ROLLS

4 fillets of whiting, 4oz(125g) grated cheese
1 small onion chopped, small knob butter
6-8 thin slices bacon, salt and pepper

Oven 375°F/190°C/Gas 5.
Cut the fillets in half lengthways; remove skin. Fry chopped onion in butter until soft. Add to cheese. Season with salt and pepper. Spread stuffing over fillets and roll up. Wrap a slice of bacon around the fish and secure with a cocktail stick. Dot with butter and bake for 20 minutes until golden brown. Serve with chips and grilled tomatoes.

BAKED TURBOT WITH SPICY SAUCE

2lb(900g) turbot
2oz(50g) butter, salt and pepper
1/2oz(12g) flour, 1/2pt(300ml) milk
2tbsp tomato pickle or chutney, 1tbsp Dijon mustard
2tbsp cream
1 lemon

Oven 375°F/190°C/Gas5.
Butter a large sheet of aluminium foil. Place the fish on the foil and dot with 1oz(25g) butter. Season with salt and pepper. Wrap neatly and bake for 15-20 minutes. Remove the black skin carefully. Make white sauce with remaining butter, flour and milk. Add tomato pickle and mustard. Bring to the boil and simmer 2 minutes. Season. Add cream and remove from heat. Arrange fish in serving dish and spoon sauce over. Serve hot garnished with parsley and lemon wedges.

SOLE VERONIQUE

1oz(25g) plus 1tsp butter
2lb(900g) Dover Sole (after skin and side bones removed)
1/2tsp salt, 1tsp black pepper
1 large onion, thinly sliced, 1tsp dried dill
8fl oz(240ml) dry white wine, 2fl oz(60ml) water
1oz(25g) flour
4fl oz(120ml) milk, 2fl oz(60ml) double cream
8oz(225g) green grapes seeded, lemon slices

Oven 400°F/200°C/Gas 6.
Grease baking dish with 1tsp butter. Rub fish with salt and pepper and arrange them on the baking dish. Sprinkle over the onion and dill. Pour on the wine and water. Bake for 8-10 minutes. Remove from the oven and transfer to a warmed serving dish. Strain the cooking liquid and reserve 4fl oz(120ml) of stock. Melt the remaining butter and add flour. Add milk and stock to make a smooth sauce. Cook for 2-3 minutes. Add cream and cook gently a further 2 minutes. Pour the sauce over the fillets, decorate with grapes and lemon slices. Serve immediately.

SOLE FILLETS WITH TOMATOES & GARLIC

2tbsp oil
1lb(450g) tomatoes, peeled, seeded and chopped
4oz(125g) canned tomato puree
2 large garlic cloves, crushed
1tsp salt, 1/4tsp black pepper, 1tsp dried oregano
2 x 11/2lb(700g) sole fish skinned and filleted
3tbsp flour, 1oz(25g) butter, 1tbsp oil
12 large black olives, stoned

Oven 350°F/180°C/Gas4.
Make the sauce - heat the oil, add tomatoes, tomato puree, garlic, Oregano, half the salt and pepper. Stir to mix, reduce heat to low, cover the pan and simmer for 30 minutes. Dip the sole fillets in seasoned flour and coat well. Fry fish for 2 minutes each side in melted butter/oil. Transfer to a warm dish. Stir olives into the sauce, pour over fish and bake for 10 minutes. Serve immediately with creamed potatoes and courgettes.
* For extra kick add chili sauce to taste to the sauce

APPLE MACKEREL

4 fresh mackerel, cleaned
1oz(25g) butter, 1tbsp oil
1 bunch spring onions, 2 sticks celery, chopped
1 apple, peeled and chopped, juice of 1 lemon
1 egg yolk, 4tbsp fresh white breadcrumbs, salt and pepper
3/4pt(450ml) dry cider
Lemon slices and parsley to garnish

Melt butter and oil in frying pan and fry onions, celery and apple until soft. Add juice of half a lemon. Remove from the heat, stir in egg yolk, breadcrumbs and seasoning. Divide this mixture in four and stuff each fish. Add dry cider and half lemon juice to frying pan and heat, stirring well. When the liquid starts to simmer, add mackerel and poach gently until cooked through. Serve garnished with a salad.

* If you prefer a crisp fish then instead of poaching fish, brush with melted butter and bake in a hot oven for 10-15 minutes.

CRISPY SMOKED FISH

11/2lb(700g) smoked fish
1 head cauliflower, 4 rashers streaky bacon
1oz(25g) flour, 1oz(25g) butter, 1tbsp oil,
3/4pt(450ml) milk
3oz(75g) grated cheese, 1oz(25g) breadcrumbs

To poach fish - place fish in cold water, bring to the boil and simmer gently for 5-7 minutes. Discard liquid. Flake fish. Chop the rashers and fry until crisp. Divide the cauliflower into florets, cook in lightly salted water until just tender. Make sauce - melt butter and oil, add flour, cook for a minute. Gradually whisk in the milk. Season. Bring the sauce to the boil, stirring. Remove from the heat and add 2oz(50g) grated cheese. Arrange the cauliflower, fish and rashers in a greased casserole dish. Pour the cheese sauce over. Mix the remaining cheese with breadcrumbs and sprinkle over the top. Heat through in a moderate oven or under the grill until the topping is crisp.

FISH PIE

1pkt puff pastry or 8oz(225g) flaky pastry
11/2lb(700g) white fish fillets
oil and butter
4 rashers streaky bacon, chopped
1 small onion, 6oz(175g) mushrooms, finely chopped
salt and pepper, pinch oregano
1/2tsp finely grated lemon rind
1tsp cornflour blended with 2fl oz(50ml) fresh cream

Oven 400°F/200°C/Gas6.
Grease a 2pt(1200ml) pie dish well with butter. Cut fillets into large pieces and place in bottom of tin. Melt a little butter and oil in a pan, add chopped bacon and cook lightly, add onion and mushrooms, fry until soft. Season with salt and pepper, few pinches oregano and lemon rind. Spread this mixture over the fish. Pour over cream and cornflour. Roll out pastry and cut out lid for pie dish. Place a strip of pastry around the wetted rim before placing on the lid. Pierce a hole in the lid and bake for 20-25 minutes.

FISH CAKES

11/2lb(750g) potatoes, peeled, boiled and mashed
12oz(350g) smoked haddock, 1/4pt(150ml) milk
1 onion, finely chopped, 3oz(75g) cheddar cheese, grated
salt and black pepper, 1 egg, beaten

CRUMB COATING

1 egg, beaten, 3oz(75g) dried breadcrumbs, 4tbsp parsley

Oven 400°F/200°C/Gas 6.
Poach the smoked haddock in a little milk until it is cooked and flakes easily. Mix the skinned, flaked fish with the other ingredients. Shape into 8-10 fingers or rounds. Chill until firm. Dip in beaten egg and then coat with breadcrumbs mixed with chopped parsley and seasoning. Place on a greased baking tray and bake for 15 minutes until golden.

FISH & CHIP PIE

1oz(25g) butter, 1tbsp oil
1 small onion, chopped
1oz(25g) flour, 1/2pt(300ml) milk
2 tomatoes, skinned and chopped
4oz(125g) frozen peas, 1tsp mixed herbs
1lb(450g) smoked cod fillets, skinned and cubed
11/2lb(700g) potatoes, peeled and cut in sticks
2tbsp oil, 1tbsp lemon juice

Oven 400°F/200°C/Gas 6.
Melt butter and oil, fry onion until soft. Stir in flour, slowly add milk and stirring well, slowly bring to the boil. Add tomatoes, peas, herbs and fish. Turn the mixture into a shallow ovenproof dish. Cook potato sticks in boiling water for 2 minutes, drain. Toss in oil and lemon juice. Arrange potato on top of fish. Bake for 20 minutes. Any fish could be used in this recipe.

* To make more filling add a layer of Cheddar cheese on top of the potato before baking

SALMON & SPINACH QUICHE

8oz(225g) shortcrust pastry
7oz(198g) can pink or red salmon, drained and skinned
2tbsp butter
1 small green pepper, de-seeded and chopped
pinch cayenne pepper, 1 small onion, chopped
8oz(225g) spinach, washed, pinch nutmeg
6oz(175g) cheddar cheese, grated
4 (size 3) eggs, beaten, 1/2pt(300ml) single cream or milk
salt and pepper, 4 tomatoes, sliced

Oven 400°F/200°C/Gas 6. Roll out pastry on a floured surface and line a 9"(23cm) metal flan tin. Line with paper and baking beans and bake `blind' for 10 minutes, remove paper and beans, cook for a further 5 minutes. Melt butter and cook pepper for 2 minutes. Remove and mix with flaked salmon and cayenne pepper. Fry onion to soften, add spinach and cook until wilted. Add nutmeg. Reserve 1oz(25g) of cheese and mix remainder with eggs and cream (or milk). Add one half of the egg mixture to the salmon and the other to the spinach. Season to taste. Spoon salmon mixture into the pastry case, bake 10 minutes until slightly set. Spoon spinach mixture on top. Reduce the oven to 350oF/180oC/ Gas 4 and bake a further 20 minutes. Arrange tomatoes on top, sprinkle with remaining cheese and bake for 5 minutes. Serve hot.

* Alternatively — omit the spinach and use 8oz of broccoli cut into small florets and par boiled (or steamed) for 5 minutes

SMOKED MACKEREL & CRAB QUICHE

PASTRY

6oz(175g) plain flour
1/2tsp curry powder, salt and freshly ground black pepper
3oz(75g) butter or margarine (frozen)
1 egg, beaten, 2-3tbsp water
1 heaped tsp wholegrain mustard

FILLING

6oz(175g) crab meat, drained
8oz(225g) `ready to eat' smoked mackerel
2 eggs plus 2 egg yolks, 1/2pt(300ml)cream
1tsp chopped parsley, 1tsp chopped chives
salt and freshly ground black pepper

Oven 350°F/180°C/Gas 4.
To make the pastry, sieve the flour, curry powder and seasoning into a bowl. Grate the butter or margarine and rub into the dry ingredients. (this can be done in a food processor) Add the egg, mustard and enough cold water to form a soft dough. Knead gently on a lightly floured board, wrap in cling film and refrigerate for at least 30 minutes. Roll out pastry and line a greased, deep-sided 8" loose-bottomed tin. Mix together the crab meat and flaked smoked mackerel. Place mixture on top of pastry base. Whisk the eggs, egg yolks, cream, herbs and seasoning together. Pour over the fish mixture. Bake in hot oven for 10 minutes, reduce the temperature to 325°F/170°C/Gas 3 and bake a further 20-25 minutes, until the filling is firm to touch. Serve warm.

PAELLA

4 chicken pieces, 2oz(50g) butter, 1tbsp oil
8oz(225g) long grain rice
1/2tsp saffron strands (or a little turmeric)
1pt(600ml) chicken stock
4oz(125g) cooked lobster meat(optional)
1 canned or bottled pimento, cut in strips
1 onion, chopped, 1 garlic clove, crushed, 1 bay leaf
6oz(175g) cooked peas, 4oz(125g) cooked prawns
8 cooked and shelled mussels

Oven 350°F/180°C/Gas 4. Skin chicken joints and fry in hot oil/butter until light brown and crisp. Remove from the pan. Cook onion and garlic until soft. Add rice and cook for one minute. Add saffron (or turmeric) to chicken stock and pour into the pan. Add bay leaf, bring to the boil and simmer gently for 10 minutes. Transfer to a large greased casserole, place chicken joints on top. Cover and cook for 15 minutes. Arrange peas, prawns, lobster, mussels, and strips of pimento over the rice and chicken. Cook in oven, uncovered for 10-15 minutes. Serve immediately.

COOK'S TIPS

Steep chicken pieces in milk for 30 minutes before use to stop them shrinking during cooking.

After flouring chicken, chill for one hour. The coating will adhere better during cooking.

Allow hot roast poultry to stand covered, in a warm place, for 10 minutes before carving.

If you find that a sauce curdles or separates when you have added cream. Remove from the heat and throw in a few ice cubes, the sauce will uncurdle.

As a change from pastry, cover a pie with a vegetable topping. Grate a raw carrot, raw parsnip and a little raw turnip. Add to this 2 cupfuls of cold mashed potato, two tablespoons of melted butter and seasoning. Mix well and spread over the pie.

To bring out the flavour of stuffing, add a 1 tsp of mustard.

If you don't have a processor to make breadcrumbs, soak cubes of bread in milk or water, squeeze out the excess liquid and crumble into the stuffing mixture.

Add a 1 tbsp of marmalade to curries to improve the flavour.

When cooking savoury rice in the microwave, add a peeled raw potato, this absorbs the excess moisture and leaves the rice fluffy.

When defrosting frozen poultry or meat, put in a colander on a plate and it will defrost more quickly.

When making a parsley sauce, add the chopped parsley after the sauce is cooked, to retain its colour and freshness. do not add the chopped parsley until the sauce has been boiled. This way the parsley will retain it's colour and freshness.

A Bouquet Garni comprises of a couple of bay leaves, a few sprigs of thyme, parsley stalks and sometimes a sprig of rosemary or sage, all tied together with cotton thread.

CHICKEN STOCK

To the skin and bones of a 3lb(1400g) chicken add:

> 2 carrots, 1 onion
> 2-3 stalks celery, 1 bay leaf
> 1 pinch thyme, 6 peppercorns
> 2 pints water

Wash bones in cold water. Chop carcass and vegetables. Put all the ingredients in a pan and bring to the boil. Simmer for 1 hour. Keep well skimmed. Strain and keep cool until ready for use.

POULTRY

LEMON CHICKEN WITH ROSEMARY

4 large chicken breasts, filleted
2tbsp plain flour
1/2tsp cumin and turmeric,
salt and black pepper
1oz(25g) butter, 2tbsp oil
1/2pt chicken stock
grated rind and juice 1 lemon
2tbsp honey, 2tsp rosemary(crushed)
roux to thicken
2tbsp cream

Place flour, cumin, turmeric, salt and pepper in a bag. Shake each chicken joint in the bag to coat. Fry the chicken in hot oil and butter until well browned. Mix together chicken stock, lemon rind, juice, honey and rosemary, add to pan, bring to boil and simmer for 15-20 minutes. Thicken with roux. Stir in cream. Serve with lemon slices and green salad.

ROSEMARY & PARMESAN -STUFFED CHICKEN

4 part-boned chicken breasts, with skin
1oz(50g) butter, softened
1oz(25g) fresh Parmesan, grated
2 garlic cloves, crushed,
2tsp fresh rosemary or 1tsp dried
6tbsp fresh breadcrumbs
2 red peppers, seeded and halved
12oz(350g) courgettes, cut into sticks
2oz(50g) black olives, 1tbsp olive oil
1/4pt(150ml) dry white wine or chicken stock, seasoning

Oven 375°F/190°C/Gas5.
Loosen the skin on the chicken breasts. Beat together the butter, garlic, Parmesan, rosemary and breadcrumbs. Season well and spread over the chicken flesh, smooth the skin back to cover the filling. Chill for 20 minutes. Cut each pepper half into three strips. Mix with the courgettes, olives, oil and seasoning. Arrange the chicken and vegetables in a single layer in a shallow ovenproof dish. Bake uncovered for 15 minutes, pour on the wine. Cook for a further 20 minutes until the chicken is cooked.

* Omit the rosemary and instead use the zest of a lemon and 2tsp fresh thyme or 1tsp dried thyme

Baked Chicken Clementine

6 chicken breasts, filleted
3oz(75g) butter, 1/2tsp ground mace,
clove garlic, crushed
3 oranges
salt and pepper
6 unsmoked, streaky rashers

SAUCE

1onion, finely chopped
2tsp flour, 2 level tsp tomato puree
1pt(600ml) chicken stock
1/2pt(300ml) dry white wine
1oz(25g) butter, 1tbsp oil
8oz(225g) small mushrooms

Oven 425°F/220°C/Gas 7.
Place each breast between two sheets of wetted greaseproof paper and gently flatten with a rolling pin. Make a savoury paste with 2oz(50g) butter, mace, garlic, the grated rind of one orange, salt and pepper. Pare the rind from the other 2 oranges, cut into inch-long threads and reserve. Remove pith from all the oranges and cut between the membranes into segments. Spread the chicken breasts with savoury paste. Put 4 or 5 segments of orange down the centre of each. Form into a roll. De-rind the bacon and stretch with a knife. Wrap bacon rashers round each breast, secure with a cocktail stick. Refrigerate for at least an hour. Melt butter in a frying pan and quickly fry chicken breasts until brown. Transfer to roasting tin - large enough to take breasts in a single layer. Bake uncovered for 20 minutes.
To make sauce: Heat the oil and gently fry onion until soft but not brown. Stir in flour and tomato puree and cook for 1 minute. Pour in stock and wine, bring to the boil, and reduce liquid by half. Blanch the orange threads in boiling water for 1min. Drain. Heat the butter and fry mushrooms for 1-2 minutes, add to the sauce, together with the orange threads. When ready to serve, arrange chicken breasts on plate, remove cocktail sticks. Add cooking liquors to sauce. Pour a little sauce over chicken with all the mushrooms and orange threads. Serve remaining sauce separately.

Chicken & Sweetcorn

4 chicken joints, 2oz(50g) seasoned flour
oil and butter for frying
2 slices bacon, 1/2pt(300ml) chicken stock
frozen sweetcorn, cornflour to thicken

Coat the chicken in the seasoned flour. Heat oil/butter and fry pieces until brown. Chop bacon and fry for few minutes. Add stock and bring to boil. Simmer 20 minutes. Add sweetcorn and simmer further 10 minutes. Thicken with cornflour if necessary.

CHICKEN CURRY

chicken pieces, 1 stock cube
2oz(50g) butter, 1tbsp oil
2 large onions, chopped, 1 clove garlic, crushed
2tbsp curry powder, 3tbsp flour
1tbsp tomato puree, 2tbsp chutney
1tbsp lemon juice, 3tsp sugar, salt and pepper
1pt(600ml) chicken stock

Cook chicken pieces in water with stock cube added until tender. Reserve stock and when cool, remove cooked chicken from bones. Cook onion and garlic in hot butter and oil until soft. Remove from heat and stir in curry powder, flour, puree, chutney, lemon juice, sugar and seasoning. Gradually blend in the stock. Bring to the boil, stirring well. Lower heat, simmer for 20 minutes stirring occasionally. Add cooked chicken and simmer for a further 15 minutes. Serve with rice or chips.

* *Any leftovers can be mixed with sufficient mayonnaise to make Coronation Chicken*

CHICKEN FRICASSEE

8 chicken portions, 3tbsp flour, salt and pepper
1lb(450g) button mushrooms, 1lb(450g) small onions
8oz(225g) rindless smoked bacon
3oz(75g) butter, 3tbsp olive oil
1/2pt(300ml) dry cider, 1/2pt(300ml) chicken stock
2 bay leaves
8 small eating apples
1tbsp Dijon mustard, 5fl oz(150ml) creme fraiche
chopped fresh parsley to garnish

Coat the chicken pieces in seasoned flour. Cover the onions with boiling water for a few minutes, drain and peel. Chop the bacon. Melt the butter in a large casserole, cook the bacon, mushrooms and onions until golden. Set aside. Add oil to the pan and brown the chicken pieces. Add the cider, stock, bay leaves, excess flour and seasoning to the chicken and bring to the boil. Lower the heat and simmer for 20 minutes. Peel and core the apples, heat the remaining butter in a frying pan and cook the apples until golden. Lower the heat, add 2tbsp water, cover the pan and cook gently for 10 minutes. Add the bacon, onions and mushrooms to the chicken, cover and cook a further 10 minutes. Skim off any excess fat. Combine the mustard, seasoning and creme fraiche, mix well. Pour over the chicken. Serve with apples and garnish with parsley.

* *Instead of apples, in season try using pears for a subtly different flavour*

GAELIC CHICKEN

4 large chicken breasts, filleted
salt and pepper, mixed herbs
1 onion, chopped, 1 clove garlic, crushed
1oz(25g) butter, 1tbsp oil
1/2tsp rosemary, 1tsp paprika, 1/2tsp curry powder
1tbsp tomato ketchup
3-4tbsp sherry, 3-4tbsp whiskey, 1/2pt(300ml) chicken stock
1tbsp cornflour or roux, 4-5 tbsp cream

Cut the chicken breasts into thick strips, season with salt, pepper and herbs. Leave aside. Melt half the butter and oil, add onion and garlic and cook until soft but not browned. Add the rosemary, paprika, curry powder, tomato ketchup, sherry, whiskey and stock. Simmer for 10 minutes. Blend the cornflour with a little water and add to the pan, stirring until thick. (or thicken with roux). Fry the chicken pieces in the remaining oil and butter until golden. Add sauce and simmer gently with a lid on for10 minutes. Stir in cream before serving with rice.

CHICKEN PAPRIKA

2lb(900g) chicken pieces
4oz(225g) mushrooms, chopped
2 stalks celery, chopped, 2 carrots, cut in strips
1 onion, thinly sliced, 1 clove garlic, crushed
1oz(25g) butter, 1tbsp oil, 1tbsp flour, 2tsp paprika
1pt(600ml) chicken stock, sour cream or plain yogurt

Oven 400°F/200°C/Gas 6.
Heat butter and oil. Fry vegetables and place in greased casserole dish. Place flour and paprika in a polythene bag, add chicken pieces and coat well. Brown chicken pieces in hot fat before placing on top of vegetables. Pour over stock, cover casserole and bake for 20-30 minutes. Stir in sour cream or yogurt. Reheat but do not boil. Serve on a bed of plain boiled rice.

* Instead of the vegetables use a can of bean (flagelot, chick pea etc), a small can of corn, and a red pepper and onion both sliced and gently fried together.

CHICKEN SUPREME

4lb(2kg) chicken cooked, 1lb broccoli, cooked
small tin condensed chicken soup
2tbsp mayonnaise, 1 clove crushed garlic(optional)
1tsp lemon juice, 2tbsp white wine
2oz grated cheese
6oz brown breadcrumbs, 1pkt potato crisps

Oven 400°F/200°C/Gas 6.
Remove the cooked meat from the chicken. In a large casserole
dish, put a layer of the cooked broccoli, then a layer of pieces of
cooked chicken. Combine the soup, mayonnaise, garlic (if
liked), lemon juice and white wine. Spoon over the chicken.
Mix the breadcrumbs, grated cheese and crushed crisps together
and shake over the top. Bake for 15-20 minutes.

** Cooked turkey slices could be used instead of chicken but as the flavour is a
bit stronger season well*

TARRAGON CHICKEN

4lb(1.8kg) chicken
1 carrot, 2 sticks celery
1/2 onion, 8 peppercorns
21/2lb(1.1kg) potatoes, salt and pepper
8oz(225g) streaky bacon
2lb(900g) leeks
12oz(350g) mushrooms
4oz(125g) butter, 1tbsp oil
4tbsp fresh or 3tsp dried tarragon
3tbsp flour
1/4pt(150ml) milk

Oven 425°F/220°C/Gas7.
Cook the chicken with carrot, celery, onion and peppercorns for
1hr 20min. Remove from the pan, leave to cool. Reduce the
stock to 1pt (600ml), strain. Par-boil the potatoes, cool, skin
and grate. Season liberally. Chop the bacon, leeks and
mushrooms. Fry the bacon until crisp, remove, fry the
mushrooms a few minutes. Melt half the butter and oil, fry the
leeks and tarragon for 5 minutes, stir in flour, cook for 1
minute, add stock and milk. Simmer until thick, season and
cool. Remove the chicken from the carcass, stir into the sauce
with the mushrooms and bacon. Spoon into a casserole dish,
cover with grated potato, drizzle with melted butter. Bake for
30 minutes.

Chicken Roulade

4 chicken breasts, boned and skinned
4 slices Blarney cheese, 4 slices lean ham
2tbsp chopped fresh parsley, salt and black pepper
1oz(25g) butter, 1tbsp oil, 1 garlic clove
1/4pt(150ml) dry white wine, 1/4pt(150ml) chicken stock
2-3tbsp fresh cream

Oven 350°F/180°C/Gas 4.
Slice the chicken breasts horizontally almost three-quarters of the way through. Open, cover with oiled greaseproof paper or clingfilm and flatten gently with a rolling pin. Place a slice of cheese and a slice of ham on top of the chicken. Sprinkle with 1tbsp parsley, season. Roll up and secure with a cocktail stick. Heat the butter/oil in a pan and fry the chicken for two minutes each side. Place the chicken pieces in a greased ovenproof dish. Combine the crushed garlic, wine and stock. Pour over the chicken. Cover and cook for 25 minutes. Pour off the sauce, strain and reduce by boiling, stir in cream. Pour the sauce around the chicken breasts, sprinkle with parsley. Serve hot.

* *Alternatively fill the chicken breasts with a thick layer of cream cheese and a rasher of cooked bacon*

Chicken & Leek Puff

6 chicken portions
2tbsp vegetable oil
2 medium leeks, cleaned and sliced
2tbsp flour
1/2pt(150ml) milk
2oz(50g) garlic and herb full-fat soft cheese
3tbsp chopped parsley
salt and pepper
1pkt puff pastry
1 egg, beaten

Oven 425°F/220°C/Gas7.
Slice the chicken into strips. Heat oil in a pan, saute the chicken for 5 minutes, add the leeks and cook for a further 3 minutes. Sprinkle flour into the pan, cook stirring continuously for 1 minute. Remove the pan from the heat and stir in the milk. Return to the heat and bring to the boil, stirring until thickened. Remove from the heat and stir in the cheese and parsley. Season to taste and leave until cold. Roll out the pastry into a rectangle and brush with beaten egg. Spoon the filling over half the pastry leaving a border around the edge. Fold the pastry over the filling, seal and crimp the edges. Make cuts in the top. Bake for 20 minutes until golden. Serve hot.

* *Alternatively use broccoli instead of leeks. Par boil the broccoli, drain and cut down into small florets. Add to the cheese and parsley sauce. Continue with the recipe as described*

Chicken & Sausage Loaf

2lb(900g) sausagemeat, 1tbsp Worcestershire sauce
2oz(50g) fresh breadcrumbs, salt and black pepper
12oz(350g) chicken breast fillets
2oz(50g) dried apricots (no soaking)
1tbsp fresh parsley, 1tbsp fresh mint, chopped
1 egg, size 4, lightly beaten
1tbsp mango chutney

Oven 350°F/180°C/Gas 4.
Grease and base line a 2lb(900g) loaf tin. Place the sausagemeat in a large bowl and mix in the Worcestershire sauce and breadcrumbs. Season with salt and pepper. Use three-quarters of the sausagemeat to line the prepared loaf tin. Cut the chicken into medium sized chunks and place in a bowl. Chop the apricots and add to the chicken with parsley, mint and beaten egg. Mix well and season. Spoon the chicken mixture into the sausage case. Cover with the remaining sausagemeat, pinching the edges to enclose filling securely. Cover tightly with greased foil. Place the loaf tin in a roasting tin with enough water in it to come halfway up the side of the loaf tin. Cook for 11/2 hours. Remove the foil and drain off any liquid. Brush the top with the mango chutney and return to the oven for 15 minutes to brown. Remove from the oven and allow to cool completely before cutting into slices.

Cold Dressed Chicken

1lb chicken breasts, boned and skinned
1 small onion, sliced, 1 bay leaf, 4 black peppercorns
1/2pt(300ml) chicken stock
7oz(200g) can tuna in brine, drained
5tbsp mayonnaise, 2tbsp lemon juice
2 red peppers, seeded and cut in thin strips
small jar of capers, pinch salt

Put the chicken breasts in a single layer in a heavy based saucepan. Add the onion, bay leaf, peppercorns and stock. Bring to the boil and reduce the heat. Cover and simmer for 15 minutes. Turn off the heat and leave the chicken to cool in the stock. Remove with a slotted spoon. Slice the breasts thickly and arrange on a serving plate. Boil the chicken stock until reduced to 5 tbsp. Strain through a fine sieve and cool. Blend the tuna, mayonnaise, lemon juice, 3tbsp stock and salt until smooth. Stir in the remaining stock to reduce the sauce to the thickness of double cream. Spoon over the chicken. Arrange the strips of red pepper in a lattice pattern on the sauce. Put a caper in the centre of each square. Chill in the refrigerator for 1 hour and serve with mixed salad and tomatoes.

TURKEY PARCELS

4 pieces of turkey breast (or chicken fillets)
1oz(25g) butter, 1tbsp oil
4 tomatoes, skinned and chopped, 1 stick celery, finely sliced
7oz(200g) can sweetcorn, 2 slices ham, chopped
salt and black pepper, 8tbsp chicken stock

Oven 375°F/190°C/Gas 5.
Cut 4 squares of tinfoil large enough to wrap around the turkey piece. Liberally grease the middle of the tinfoil. Rub the turkey with butter. Season and place the turkey pieces on the tinfoil. Mix the vegetables and ham together and divide between the 4 pieces of turkey. Spoon the stock over each parcel and fold the foil over to enclose tightly. Set in a roasting tin and bake for 45 minutes.
Alternative filling — cut up 6 pieces of streaky bacon, with 1 small cut and fried onion. 4oz chopped walnuts and 4oz brown breadcrumbs. Mix together. Follow recipe. Serve with cranberry sauce

STUFFED TURKEY ESCALOPES

4 x 4oz(100g) turkey escalopes
2oz(25g) butter, 1tbsp oil
1 onion, finely chopped
1oz(25g) streaky bacon, finely chopped
1oz(25g) mushrooms, finely chopped
1tbsp chopped fresh parsley
2oz(50g) fresh white breadcrumbs
2tbsp grated Parmesan cheese
salt and pepper
1 egg, size 3, beaten
2tbsp plain flour
1/4pt(150ml) white wine
1/4pt(150ml) chicken stock
salt and pepper

Oven 350°F/180°C/Gas 4.
Flatten out escalopes between two sheets clingfilm or greaseproof paper. Season well. Make stuffing:- melt half the butter and oil in a small pan, fry onion and bacon until lightly browned. Add mushrooms and cook until moisture has gone. Leave to cool for 5 minutes and then mix in parsley, breadcrumbs, and cheese. Season and add enough egg to bind mixture. Divide the stuffing into four and place at one end of escalope. Roll them up and secure closed with cocktail sticks. Heat remaining butter and oil and fry rolls until browned evenly. Place in a greased roasting dish, spoon 4tbsp wine over the rolls. Cover and roast for 1 hour. Place on a heated dish and remove the cocktail sticks. Stir flour into pan juices and gradually add the remaining wine and stock. Simmer for 3-4 minutes and pour sauce over the escalopes.

TURKEY BOURGUIGNON

1oz(25g) butter, 1tbsp oil
2lb(900g) turkey breast, cut in slices
4oz(100g) streaky bacon
8oz(225g) onions, peeled and chopped
1oz(25g)flour, 1/2pt(300ml) stock, 1/2pt(300ml) red wine
1 clove garlic crushed, salt and pepper, 1 bouquet garni
12 small onions, 6oz(175g) mushrooms

Oven 375°F/190°C/Gas 5.
Heat oil and butter, fry turkey slices until golden brown.
Remove from pan and place in an ovenproof casserole dish. De-rind and chop bacon, fry until crisp, add onions and garlic, cook until soft, add flour and fry for a few seconds. Blend in water and wine, seasoning and the bouquet garni. Bring to the boil stirring constantly. Pour over the turkey, cover with lid and bake for 40 minutes. Add onions and mushrooms and cook for a further half hour. Serve with boiled rice or potatoes.

PEACHY DUCK

4 duck breasts
14oz(400g) can peach halves in natural juice
1/4pt(150ml) red wine, rind and juice 2 oranges
1tbsp Worcestershire sauce, 1/2tsp garlic salt
salt and pepper
1/4pt(150ml) sour cream

Oven 400°F/200°C/Gas 6.
Drain the peaches and mix the juice with red wine, Worcestershire sauce, garlic salt, orange rind and juice in a shallow dish. Prick the duck breasts through with a skewer. With a sharp knife cut a pocket in each breast, being careful not to cut right through. Insert half a peach inside the pocket and close the meat together with a cocktail stick. Lay the breasts in the marinade and chill for two hours, turning the breasts after an hour. Remove and dry with a paper towel. Season with salt and pepper and lay in a greased baking tin, skin side upwards. Roast for 35 minutes. Finely chop any remaining peaches and add to the marinade. Skim fat from duck juices and add to the marinade. Pour all the liquid into a saucepan, bring to the boil, fast boil to reduce by half. Remove from the heat and whisk in soured cream. Heat through without boiling. Serve sauce with the duck breasts.

CHINESE CRISPY DUCK

5lb(2.2kg) Duck
Vegetable oil for deep frying
Soy and Herb Sauce
11/2pt(900ml) water
1/3pt(200ml) soy sauce
5oz(115g) sugar
2 cloves garlic, crushed, 2 slices root ginger
Bouquet Garni
1 large onion, sliced

Put garlic, ginger and Bouquet Garni in a muslin bag. Mix rest of ingredients and bring to the boil. Add muslin bag and simmer for 30 minutes. Remove muslin bag and sauce is ready for use. Cut the duck into pieces. Place in a pan of boiling water and simmer for 10 minutes. Remove and wipe dry. Bring soy and herb sauce to the boil and cook duck pieces in this for 45 minutes. Remove and dry well. The duck will now be very brown. Heat cooking oil, then using a basket, lower duckling pieces into the hot oil and cook until skin is crispy. Remove and drain well. Thicken sauce with cornflour and serve with duck.

DUCK WITH ORANGE SAUCE

1 Duck (allow 11/4lb(600g) per person)
orange marmalade
grated rind and juice 2 oranges
2tbsp dry red wine, 1/2 wine glass of sherry
2tbsp redcurrant jelly, 2 oranges, sliced

Oven 425°F/220°C/Gas7.
Make stock with giblets. Place the duck on a trivet in a roasting tin and prick all over with a fork. Season liberally with salt and pepper. Put into the hot oven for 20 minutes then reduce heat to 350oF/180oC/Gas4. Roast for 25 minutes per 1lb(450g) weight. Remove the tin from the oven and pour off the fat (reserve this for roasting potatoes). Leave the duck to rest for 5 minutes. Cut the duck into four portions (kitchen scissors are useful for cutting the duck) and place on a lightly greased tray. Cover the portions liberally with marmalade and return to hot oven for10-15 minutes. To make the sauce:- deglaze the roasting tin with a little stock and pour into a saucepan. Add rind and juice of oranges, wine, sherry and redcurrant jelly. Stir until jelly is dissolved and bring to the boil. Season to taste. The sauce can be thickened with roux if required. Serve the duck pieces with sauce and orange slices.

STUFFING FOR ROAST DUCK

1 large chopped onion
1/2tsp ground bay leaf, 1tsp thyme and parsley
1tbsp raisins, 1 cooking apple, chopped
butter and oil
14oz(400g) soft white breadcrumbs, salt and black pepper
1 egg, size 3

Melt butter and oil and fry chopped onions with bay leaf, thyme and parsley. Add raisins and cooking apple and cook for a few minutes. Add breadcrumbs, season and combine the ingredients with beaten egg. Wrap in buttered foil in a long tube, cook in hot oven for 15-20 minutes. Slice and serve with roast duck.

PHEASANT WITH PORT

Marinade - 1/2pt(300ml) red wine, 2tbsp port, 1tbsp
olive oil, 1tsp mustard, 1tsp coriander seeds
1tsp grated orange rind, black pepper
2-3 young pheasants, well wiped and skinned
2tbsp vegetable oil
/2pt(300ml) chicken stock, 8tbsp port
Finely grated rind and juice of 2 oranges
2oz(50g) sultanas
salt and black pepper, 2tbsp cornflour

Oven 350°F/180°C/Gas 4.
Leave the pheasants in the marinade overnight, turn them over a few times. Discard the marinade, dry the pheasants and brown in oil. Place in a casserole dish, add the remaining ingredients except the cornflour. Cook for 1 hour basting regularly. Thicken the sauce with cornflour and serve the pheasant in portions.

A GUIDE TO THE FRYING TIME FOR STEAKS

The following guide gives the frying time for different steaks. Grilling time would be a little longer. Turn the steaks half way through cooking.

Fillet: the tenderest of steaks from the undercut of sirloin, but lacks some of the flavour of rump. Cut 11/2"(7.5cm) thick.
Rare 6 minutes; medium to well done 8-10 minutes.

Tournedos: Little round steaks sliced from the fillet and tied in neat shapes. Grill or saute very rapidly. Cut 1"(2.5cm) thick.
Rare 5 minutes, medium to well done 6-8 minutes.

Chateaubriand: Cut from centre of fillet. Cut 2"(5cm) thick and weighs 12-14oz(350-400g)- serves two people. Rare 10-15 minutes; medium rare 16-20 minutes; well done 25 minutes.

T-bone: Cut directly across the sirloin. Cut 11/2-2"(3.5-5cm) thick.
Rare 7-8 minutes; medium 8-10minutes; well done 12-15 minutes.

Sirloin: like T-bone but without the bone.

Porterhouse: Cut from the wing rib. Cut 11/2"(3.5cm) thick.
Rare 7 minutes; medium rare 9-10 minutes; well done 12 minutes.

Entrecote (Ribsteak): cut from between two wing ribs, or upper part of sirloin. Tender with fine flavour. Has a little more fat that other steaks. Cut 3/4"(15mm) thick.
Rare 5 minutes; medium 6-7 minutes; well done 9-10 minutes.

Rump Steak: firm texture, excellent flavour. Cut 1"(2.5cm) thick.
Rare 6-7 minutes; medium 9-11 minutes; well done 14-16 minutes.

Minute: A thin slice of entrecote or fillet. Cut 1/2"(10mm) thick.
Rare 3 minutes; medium 5 minutes; well done 7-8 minutes.

BEEF

CHUMP SAVOURY

2lb(450g) chump, sirloin or fillet steak
2 medium onions, 8oz(225g) mushrooms
8oz(225g) green beans, 8 small tomatoes
4tbsp soy sauce, 4tbsp water, 4tbsp red wine
seasoning, oil/butter for frying

Cut steak into very fine 2"(5cm) strips. Slice onions and mushrooms thinly. Quarter tomatoes. Heat the oil in large pan and brown the meat quickly on both sides. Add remaining ingredients, cover and simmer for about 8-10 minutes. Serve immediately.

BEEF SUPREME

2lb(900g) beef steak in two fillets, one larger than
the other, French mustard, 6 rindless rashers bacon
1oz(25g) butter, 1tbsp vegetable oil
1/4pt(150ml) red wine

FILLING

4oz(125g) herb and garlic cream cheese
3oz(75g) cream cheese
1tsp dried tarragon, 1tsp chopped parsley
1 onion, finely chopped, 1 large egg, beaten
6tbsp dried breadcrumbs, salt and black pepper

Oven 375°F/190°C/Gas 5.
Make filling - cook the onion in a little butter and oil until soft. Cool and combine with all other ingredients. Spread a thin layer of mustard on one side of each steak. Place 3 rashers on the larger steak. Spread the filling over the bacon and then place the remaining rashers on top. Place the smaller steak on top - mustard side down. Tie the steaks securely together with string. Brown the meat evenly in hot oil/butter in a pan. Place a large square of tin foil in a roasting tin. Place the steak in the centre. Fold up the foil around the steak. Pour the wine into the pan and stir to remove any sediment or juices.

Pour over the meat. Close the foil securely at the top. Cook for 50 minutes, open the foil and cook a further 15 minutes. Take the meat from the oven and allow to stand for 2-3 minutes. Pour off the juices into a saucepan. Spoon a few tablespoons of juice over the meat. Thicken the remaining juices and add more wine and seasoning if desired. (The cooking time depends on the thickness of the meat and one's preference - for rare beef - 30 minutes cooking and 10 minutes with foil open would be sufficient).

SIRLOINS IN FOIL

4 x 8oz(225g) sirloin steaks, 4oz(125g) mushrooms, sliced
1 medium onion, chopped, 4 tomatoes, sliced
a little red wine (optional), salt and pepper, 1tbsp oil

Oven 350°F/180°C/Gas 4.
Cut 4 squares of tinfoil large enough to wrap around each steak.
Chop mushrooms, onions and tomatoes finely. Heat oil in a
frying pan over a high heat and brown the steaks for one
minute each side. Place each steak on a piece of foil. Add
vegetables to the pan and fry for a few minutes. Divide mixture
over each steak. Season. (Add a dash of wine if using). Wrap
securely in the foil and bake for 20 minutes.

GAELIC STEAKS

1 large carrot, 2 onions, chopped
2tbsp chopped parsley, 1/2tbsp fresh thyme, 1 bay leaf
1oz(25g) butter, 1tbsp oil, 1/4pt(150ml) white wine
1/4pt(150ml) beef stock, 1tbsp tomato puree
6 fillet or rump steaks
8oz(225g) mushrooms, halved
2tbsp Irish whiskey, salt and black pepper
*1tbsp Worcester sauce, 1tsp coarse grain mustard_*
1/2pt(300ml) fresh cream

Make the sauce - fry the 1 onion and carrot in hot oil/butter.
Add 1tbsp parsley, thyme, bayleaf, wine, stock and tomato
puree. Simmer for 30 minutes. Sieve and keep warm. Heat a
pan with 1tbsp oil added. Brown the steaks quickly and cook
for 7- 8 minutes. Remove from the pan and keep warm. Add
pan juices to sauce. Put a knob of butter and a little oil in the
pan, fry remaining onion until soft, add mushrooms and 1tbsp
parsley. Cook a further minute. Return the steaks to the pan,
heat through. Pour whiskey over the steaks and set alight.
Cover the pan after 10 seconds to put the flames out. Arrange
the steaks on a heated serving plate. Stir the sauce into the
mushroom mixture. Stir in cream. Reheat without boiling. Add
seasoning, mustard and Worcester sauce to taste. Pour around
the steak and serve garnished with parsley.

STEAK & KIDNEY PIE

1 1/2lb(700g) lean stewing beef
8oz(225g) lamb's kidney
3tbsp oil, 1 onion, chopped
1/2pt(300ml) beef stock
1/2pt(300ml) stout, 1tbsp Worcestershire Sauce
6oz(175g) button mushrooms
roux to thicken sauce, salt and black pepper
1lb(450g) puff or flaky pastry

Cut the steak in 1"(2.5cm) pieces. Wash and dry the kidneys, peel off the membrane and discard. Using scissors, cut the kidneys in halves or thick slices. Remove the white core from the centre, wash well again and dry thoroughly. Heat 2tbsp oil and add the meat and kidneys, cook until well browned on all sides. Remove the meat from the pan and add the onion, cook gently for a few minutes until softened. Return the meat to the pan, add stock, stout and sauce. Cover pan and simmer for 1 1/2 hours until the meat is tender. Season to taste and add roux to thicken sauce. Heat the remaining oil in a pan, add the mushrooms, saute for a few minutes. Stir into the meat. Oven 400oF/200oC/Gas6. Transfer the meat to a oval 2pt(1.2ltr) ovenproof pie dish. Place a pie-funnel or an old porcelain egg cup in the centre of the dish. Roll out the pastry and cut an oval 2"(5cm) larger than the pie dish. Cut a thin strip from around the edge of the oval. Moisten the rim of the dish and place the pastry on it. Moisten the pastry rim with a little water. Cut a small hole in the centre of the pastry lid and gently place it over the pie dish. Press around the edges to seal, trim any excess and knock up and flute the edge with your finger and a small knife. Use the pastry trimmings to make leaves for decoration. Bake for 15 minutes, Remove from the oven and glaze with beaten egg. Return to the oven for a further 10 minutes until well risen and golden brown.

BEEF STROGANOFF

1oz(25g) butter, 1tbsp oil
1 1/2lb(700g) braising steak, cut in thin strips
1 large onion, sliced
10oz(298g) can condensed cream of chicken soup
1/2 soup can water, 4tbsp white wine
4oz(125g) mushrooms, 1/4pt(150ml) soured cream or
yoghurt

Stir-fry meat in hot butter and oil until well browned. Remove meat and add onions and fry until soft. Add soup, water and wine, mix well. Bring to the boil and return meat to pan. Cover and simmer gently for 40 minutes. Add mushrooms and cook for a further 20 minutes. Add cream or yoghurt just before serving. Reheat but do not boil.

* For a hotter Stroganoff add 1tsp of chili powder or chili sauce to the soup and water mix

STOUT BEEF

2lb(900g) lean stewing beef, seasoned flour
2oz(50g) butter, 2tbsp oil
2 thinly sliced onions
2tsp sugar, 1tsp mustard powder
1tbsp tomato puree, 1 strip dried orange peel
bouquet garni, 1pt(600ml) stout
8oz(225g) mushrooms, salt and black pepper

Oven 300°F/150°C/Gas2.
Cut the meat into 11/2"(3.5cm) cubes and toss in seasoned flour. Heat half the oil and butter, fry meat in batches until brown. Transfer to casserole dish, add more oil and fry onion. Deglaze with stout. Add sugar, mustard, tomato puree, orange rind, bouquet garni and seasoning. Bring to the boil and simmer in low oven for 2 - 21/2 hours. Saute mushrooms in a little melted butter and oil. Season and add to cooked stew. Simmer a further 2-3 minutes.

PAUPIETTES DE BOEUF

6 slices topside beef, 8oz(225g) pork sausage meat
salt and pepper, dried or fresh rosemary
1oz(25g) butter, 1tbsp oil
1 large onion, chopped, 8oz(225g) mushrooms, sliced
1lb(450g) tomatoes, peeled and sliced
3tbsp red wine, 1tbsp cornflour

Oven 325°F/160°C/Gas 3.
Spread the slices of beef with sausage meat, season lightly and add a little crushed rosemary. Roll up and secure with a cocktail sticks. Heat butter and oil and fry rolls until evenly browned. Drain on kitchen paper. Reheat fat and add onion and mushrooms, cook for 3 minutes. Place the vegetables on the base of a greased, rectangle, ovenproof dish. Add three-quarters of the tomatoes. Lay beef rolls, side by side on top. Add red wine and season. Cover with a tight-fitting lid, simmer on top of cooker for 11/2 hours or in the oven for 2 hours. Thicken the juices with cornflour, blended with a little water. Adjust seasoning. Add remaining tomatoes. Reheat, garnish with rosemary. Serves 4-6.

* To the sausage meat add 3oz chopped dried apricots and 2oz of chopped almonds, season but omit the rosemary

SWISS STEAK

11/2lb(700g) topside of beef
11/2oz(40g) flour, salt and black pepper
1oz(25g) butter, 1tbsp oil
2 onions, finely sliced, 2 sticks celery, chopped
8oz(225g) can chopped tomatoes, 1/4pt(150ml) beef stock
2tsp tomato puree, 1tsp Worcestershire sauce

Oven to 300ºF/150ºC/Gas 2.
 Cut the steak into eight pieces. Season the flour with salt and pepper. Press the pieces of steak into the flour so that it is well covered - use all the flour. Heat the butter/oil in a pan, brown the meat quickly on both sides. Transfer the meat to a greased casserole dish. Add the onion and celery to the pan, fry until soft. Add to the casserole with tomatoes, tomato puree, stock and Worcestershire sauce. Cover casserole and cook for 21/2 hours until meat is tender. (Or cook in a saucepan on top of cooker)

BEEF CASSEROLE

3lb(1400g) beef rump
6oz(175g) belly of pork, skinned and diced
2oz(50g) butter, 3tbsp oil
2 onions, chopped, 2 garlic cloves, crushed
9fl oz(270ml) red wine, 1/4pt(150ml) dry martini
1/2beef stock cube, 1tsp dried thyme, 1 bay leaf
1tbsp tomato puree, strip of orange peel, seasoning

Oven 275ºF/140ºC/Gas 1.
Blanch the pork in boiling water for 4-5 minutes. Trim and cut the meat into large chunks. Heat oil in large pan, fry onion and garlic until soft. Fry the beef in two lots until evenly browned. Return all beef to pan with vegetables and pork. Heat wine until boiling and add to the pan with martini. Dissolve the stock cube in 1/2pt(300ml) water and add to meat with herbs, orange peel and tomato puree. Season well. Cover and cook for 2 hours. Serves 6.

MEAT LOAF

11/2lb(700g) minced stewing beef
8oz(225g) minced pork
1 large onion, finely chopped, 2 cloves garlic, crushed
8oz(225g) mushrooms, chopped
1tbsp plain flour
4oz(125g) oatmeal or wholemeal bread crumbs
salt and black pepper, 1/2tsp nutmeg
1tbsp chopped fresh parsley, 1tsp mixed herbs
2tbsp soy sauce, 1tbsp tomato ketchup
2 large eggs, beaten
1oz(25g) butter and a little oil

Oven 375ºF/190ºC/Gas5.
2lb loaf tin, greased and base lined.Melt butter and oil in a pan and fry onion and garlic until soft, add chopped mushrooms and fry until soft. Put the meats in a large dish, add the mushroom mixture and the remaining ingredients. Mix well. Put into a well greased loaf tin. Bake for 45 minutes, reduce to 350oF/180oC/Gas4 for a further 30-35 minutes. Serves 6.

SAVOURY PUFF SLICE

1lb(450g)pkt puff pastry
8oz(225g)pkt frozen mixed vegetables
2oz(50g) cheddar cheese, grated
2tbsp chutney, left-over meat loaf

Oven 400°F/200°C/Gas 6.
Grease a 7 x 11 Swiss roll tin. Cut the meat loaf into 1"(2.5cm) slices. Roll out half the pastry on a floured work surface and use to line the tin. Spread the pastry with chutney and sprinkle vegetables over the top. Arrange the sliced meat loaf over the vegetables and sprinkle with grated cheese. Roll out the rest of the pastry and place over meat. Seal edges and make cuts across the top. Bake for 30 minutes until golden. Serves 4-6

COTTAGE PIE

1lb(450g) stewing beef, minced
1 onion, chopped, 1 clove garlic, crushed
1tbsp Worcester sauce, 1tbsp Mushroom Ketchup
1/2pt(300ml) beef stock or gravy, dash red wine
1 carrot and 1 stick celery, chopped small
salt and black pepper, roux made with flour
1oz(25g)butter, 1tbsp oil
cooked potatoes, seasoning, fresh cream and milk

Cook the onion and garlic in hot oil and butter for a few minutes until soft, add mince and brown lightly. Add stock, wine and sauces. Bring to the boil and simmer for 40 minutes. Add carrot and celery pieces, cook a further 10 minutes. Thicken the dish with roux. Boil potatoes in their jackets. When cooked, peel and season with salt, pepper and onion salt. Add fresh cream and milk and mash well.

Oven 350oF/180oC/Gas 4. Put the mince into a casserole dish. Cover with the mashed potato. Sprinkle the top with some crushed potato crisps and bake in the oven until the top is crisp. Leftover minced roast beef can be substituted for some of the fresh mince.

BASIC BEEFBURGERS

1lb(450g) minced beef or pork, 3oz(75g) bread crumbs
1tsp dried parsley, 1tsp dried thyme or mixed herbs
1 clove garlic crushed (optional), pepper and 1tsp salt
1 large egg, beaten, 1tbsp oil

Combine the first five (or six) ingredients together with egg. Shape with lightly floured hands into six 3"(7.5cm) burgers. Heat oil in frying pan and fry burgers for 10 minutes each side with pan covered. Alternatively burgers can be grilled. When shaping the burgers, wrap meat tightly around the cheese. Shape as usual and chill well for 20 minutes.

LASAGNE

1oz(25g) butter, 1tbsp oil
4 slices streaky bacon, finely chopped
1 large onion, finely chopped, 2 cloves garlic, crushed
11/2lb(700g) lean minced beef
2tbsp flour
3tbsp tomato puree, 1 x 14oz(400g)tin chopped tomatoes
1/2pt(300ml) beef stock, 1/4pt(150ml) red wine
1tsp mixed herbs or basil, salt and pepper
10oz(275g) ready cooked lasagne sheets

CHEESE SAUCE

1oz(25g) butter, 1tbsp oil
2oz(50g) flour, 3/4pt(450ml) milk
1/4pt(150ml) cream
2oz(50g) cheddar cheese, grated
pinch nutmeg, salt and pepper

Oven 350°F/180°C/Gas 4.
Cook the bacon pieces in hot oil/butter until crisp. Add onion
and garlic and cook until soft. Stir in meat and brown well.
Add tomatoes, puree, stock, herbs, and seasoning. Bring to the
boil, reduce heat and simmer gently for 20 minutes. Stir
occasionally to avoid the meat sticking to the bottom of the
pan. Cool and remove any fat from the top, add flour to this fat
and stir into the dish to thicken the sauce.
Cheese sauce - melt oil and butter in a saucepan. Add flour and
make a roux. Slowly add milk and stirring, bring gently to the
boil. Remove from heat and add cream, cheese, nutmeg and
seasoning. Stir until cheese has melted. Butter a large, rectangle
baking dish. Spread half the meat sauce over the base, cover
with sheets of lasagne. Spread half the cheese sauce on top.
Repeat layers ending with cheese sauce. A little extra cheese can
be grated on top if desired. Bake for 40 minutes until browned.
Serve with green salad and garlic bread. This dish can be
prepared in advance and if left standing for over 1 hour, the
cooking time can be reduced by 10 minutes. Serves 6.

Roast Beef

Beef on the bone will have much more flavour than that roasted off the bone. Ask the butcher to cut through the upper chine bone so that the 'feather bones' can be removed easily before carving. If liked you can have half of the ribs cut off and cook this cut separately.

Rib of Roast, on the Bone
(8-10OZ PER PERSON)

seasoning and coarse grain mustard
crushed garlic, chopped parsley
onion and garlic skins, carrot or parsnip peelings
cooking oil

Oven 450°F/230°C/Gas 8.
Cut a line between the fat and the 'feather bones' to facilitate the fat shrinkage. Put the piece of roast on a plate, rub the fat with a little oil. Cover lightly with coarse grain mustard. Liberally season with freshly ground black pepper, herb pepper and crushed garlic. Some parsley can also be sprinkled on top. Leave for 4-5 hours or overnight. Put some oil in a large roasting tin, brown the meat to seal. Remove meat and put in the skins and peelings, then put a rack or wire tray on top. Put meat on the rack and place in a hot oven for 20 minutes. Lower heat to 350°F/180°C/Gas 4 for remainder of cooking time. Roasting times will vary according to your oven but a rough guide is:

Rare 12 - 15 minutes per 1lb(450g)
Medium 15 - 18 minutes per 1lb(450g)
Well done 18 - 20 minutes per 1lb(450g)
These times include the 20 minutes in the hot oven.

When the meat is cooked it can be tested with a skewer to see the colour of the juices, if these are bloody then the meat is rare. Remove the meat onto a warm plate, cover with tinfoil and leave in a warm place for half an hour. Remove the feather bones and one rib at the time before carving.

To make gravy - pour off any fat from the roasting tin, this can be used for roasting vegetables. Add some water to the tin and stir well to de-glaze. Strain this liquid into a saucepan. Add more water and stir again to remove all the sediment. Strain this into the saucepan.

Discard the peelings. The liquid in the saucepan should be a nice brown colour, add half a beef stock cube and a good dash of red wine. Bring to the boil, stir well and simmer 10-15 minutes, add any juices seeped from the resting meat. Taste for seasoning. Serve in a gravy boat. If liked this sauce can be thickened with a little roux.

BEARNAISE SAUCE TO SERVE WITH STEAK

4tbsp tarragon vinegar, 4tbsp dry white wine
2tsp finely chopped shallots, pinch ground black pepper
1tbsp French tarragon leaves
3 egg yolks, 1tsp mustard powder, 6oz(175g) butter,

If tarragon vinegar is unavailable use wine vinegar and add extra fresh tarragon. Boil the first four ingredients together until almost completely reduced. Add 1tbsp cold water immediately. Remove the pan from the heat and allow to cool for 1-2 minutes, whisk in the egg yolks and mustard powder. Add the butter bit by bit over a low heat, whisking continuously. As soon as one piece melts add the next until the sauce thickens. (If it becomes too thick remove from the heat and add a little cold water or place the saucepan in a bowl of cold water) Finally add the chopped tarragon and taste for seasoning. If the saucepan feels too hot for your hand then it is too hot for the sauce. Keep the sauce warm over a bowl of warm water or in a thermos flask.

MUSHROOM CREAM SAUCE

2oz(50g) butter, 1 onion, chopped
3oz(50g) mushrooms, sliced
1/4pt(150ml) chicken stock
2tbsp dry white wine, 1tsp lemon juice
roux, 1/4pt(150ml) fresh cream, salt and pepper

Heat the butter in pan then add onion and mushrooms, cook until tender. Add the chicken stock, wine and lemon juice, simmer for a few minutes. Thicken with roux, simmer for 2 minutes. Add cream and seasoning. Process or liquidise the sauce - it does not have to be smooth. Serve hot.

TOMATO SAUCE

1oz(25g) butter
6 tomatoes. peeled, de-seeded and chopped
2tbsp chopped parsley, salt and black pepper

Melt butter in a pan, add the tomatoes, parsley and pan juices. Season. Stir well and heat through before serving.

*Change the flavour with a few drops of either Worcestershire sauce, a couple of spoonfuls of horseradish or chilli sauce.

Cuts of Lamb

Breast - this cut inclines to be fatty. Boned, excess fat removed and stuffed this cut is a very economical and tasty joint for roasting.

Scrag end of Neck- usually cut in rounds, suitable for soups and stews.

Middle neck of Lamb - Cut in chops, can be grilled or fried. Also can be used in casseroles or stews.

Lamb Fillet- this is the meat boned out of the neck of lamb into a long fillet. It is ideal for grilling or roasting.

Best end of Neck - this can be roasted whole or cut into cutlets for frying or grilling. It can be boned and rolled and cut into 'noisettes' or boned, rolled and stuffed and used as a roasting joint. Two of these cuts can be used to make `Crown Roast' or a `Guard of Honour`

Loin - the whole piece can be boned, stuffed and rolled as used as a roasting joint. The loin can be cut into loin or chump chops.

Shoulder - has quite a lot of fat. The bone can be removed and the joint stuffed for roasting. This cut is often divided into smaller joints, the blade and knuckle end.

Leg - this is the prime cut for roasting. It can be purchased whole or cut into `best end' and the `knuckle end'. The `best end' can be boned and cut for lamb cutlets.

Liver - this can be grilled, fried or baked.

Cooks Tips

For thin slices of whole liver, pour boiling water over it, leave for a minute, drain and dry. It will slice easily with a sharp knife.

Marinade liver in milk for an hour before use, it will be more tender and easily cooked.

Before roasting lamb, tuck bits of garlic and rosemary into small holes in the skin, to improve the flavour.

The way you prepare and cook garlic affects the flavour and smell. If you want a delicate flavour, leave the cloves whole or just rub round the dish with a cut clove. For a stronger taste add chopped garlic, and for a very strong flavour, crush the cloves.

$\mathcal{L}$AMB

ROAST LEG OF LAMB

First remove the `aitch` bone for easier carving. Rub the skin with oil, stab holes in the fat with the point of a knife and push sprigs of fresh rosemary and garlic into them. Season liberally with black pepper and herb pepper. Leave 4-5 hours or overnight and roast as for beef with the vegetables peelings in the base of the tin. When making the gravy use the same ingredients as for the beef gravy but add some redcurrant jelly to give a lovely flavour.

STUFFING FOR
BONED LEG OF LAMB

6oz(175g) fresh white breadcrumbs
1 onion, finely chopped
2oz(50g) butter, 1tsp oil
2oz(50g) no-soak apricots
1 carrot, finely grated
1tbsp chopped parsley, 1tsp chopped fresh rosemary
salt and black pepper
1 egg, size 3

Melt all the butter and oil, fry the onion until soft but not coloured. Meanwhile place all the remaining ingredients except the egg in a bowl. Add the onion and butter, mix well. Beat the egg and add to the bowl, mix well to combine.

* Instead of breadcrumbs use 6oz swollen couscous with 2oz of sultanas. Leave out the carrot but otherwise proceed with the recipe

SPICED MARINATED LAMB

6lb leg of lamb
6 large cloves garlic, 2"(5cm) piece root ginger, peeled
2tsp sea salt, grated rind and juice of 1 lemon
1 heaped tsp cumin powder, 1/2tsp dried cloves
1/2tsp ground turmeric, 1tsp dried rosemary
1pt natural yoghurt, 11/2tsp honey

Oven 425°F/220°C/Gas 7.
Using a skewer make small holes all over the surface of the lamb. Put the first 8 ingredients into a blender and puree until smooth. Rub over the lamb and place on a dish. Add half the yoghurt and honey to the blender, process and pour over the lamb. Refrigerate overnight. Cover with foil, cook for 1 hour. Remove the foil, cook a further 30 minutes. Stir remaining yoghurt into the pan juices and serve with sliced lamb.

POTATO-WRAPPED LAMB

1lb(450g) potatoes
2 x 8oz(225g) lamb fillets, 1 garlic clove, 2tbsp oil
1tbsp chopped fresh rosemary, salt and pepper
1 egg, size 3, beaten, 1oz(25g) butter, melted
rosemary leaves to garnish

Oven 350°F/180°C/Gas 4.
Peel the potatoes and boil in salted water for 8 minutes. Drain in a colander and leave aside to go cold. Trim the fat from the lamb and make small deep incisions all over the meat with a sharp knife. Cut the clove of garlic into slivers and poke a piece into each incision. Heat oil in a pan and lightly brown the meat on all sides. Make the potato crust by coarsely grating the potatoes into a large bowl. Using a fork, stir in the rosemary and season to taste. Add enough egg to moisten mixture. Lay the fillets on an oiled baking sheet and gently mould the potato mixture over each one. Brush with melted butter and cook for 45 minutes. Serve garnished with rosemary leaves. [One 8oz(225g) lamb fillet will serve 2 people].

* Flavour the potato mix with 1 tbsp of chopped mint instead of rosemary. Garnish with mint

ROSTI - TOPPED LAMB HOTPOT

2tbsp olive oil, 1lb(450g) lamb pieces
1 onion, peeled and sliced, 1 small aubergine, cubed
6oz (175g) courgettes, sliced
1 red pepper, de-seeded and cut into large dice
14 oz(395g) plum tomatoes, 2tbsp sun-dried tomato
paste1/4pt(150ml) red wine
1tbsp mint and rosemary seasoning
roux for thickening
1lb(450g) potatoes, 3tbsp olive oil
spicy garlic chip seasoning

Oven 400°F/200°C/Gas 6.
Heat oil in a pan and fry lamb pieces to seal. Add vegetables, cook for 5 minutes. Stir in tomatoes, juice, tomato paste, wine and seasoning. Bring to the boil and simmer for 40 minutes. Thicken with roux. Spoon into a casserole dish. Coarsely grate potatoes, rinse under cold water and pat dry. Place in a mixing bowl with olive oil and seasoning, mix well, spoon over the lamb. Bake for 30 minutes until golden.

* Instead of grated potato cover the lamb with a thick layer of corn chips (eg 'ordinary' or cheese flavour). Bake for about 20 minutes being careful that the chips don't burn

RATATOUILLE & LAMB BAKE

2tbsp oil, 4 lean lamb chops
1 clove garlic, crushed, 1 large onion, sliced
1 red pepper, sliced, 1 aubergine, sliced
1lb(450g) courgettes, sliced
1lb(450g) potatoes, sliced
1lb(450g) fresh tomatoes or 14oz(400g) can tomatoes
salt and pepper

Place slices of aubergine on a plate and shake salt over them, leave for 15 minutes, rinse off salt and pat dry with kitchen paper. Brown the lamb chops on both sides in hot oil. Remove from the pan and leave aside. Add the garlic and onion and cook until soft. Add red pepper, prepared aubergine, courgettes and potatoes, stir well. Add the chopped fresh tomatoes and seasoning. Return the chops to the pan, cover with lid and simmer gently, stirring occasionally, for 25-30 minutes until vegetables are tender and meat is cooked.

LAMB & MUSHROOM KORMA

1oz(25g) butter, 1tbsp oil
1 large onion, chopped, 2 cloves garlic, crushed
1tbsp fresh root ginger, grated
1tsp turmeric, 1tsp ground cumin, 1tsp ground coriander
1 fresh chilli, de-seeded and chopped
3-4 cardamom pods, de-seeded and crushed
2lb(1kg) lean lamb, cubed
1/4pt(125ml) natural yoghurt, mixed with 1tsp cornflour
8oz(225g) mushrooms, sliced
1tbsp lemon or lime juice
salt and black pepper

Melt the butter and oil and saute the onion until soft, add garlic and spices and fry for 2 minutes. Add lamb pieces and coat well in the spice mixture. Stir in yoghurt, cover and simmer gently for 45 minutes, stirring occasionally. Add mushrooms and cook a further 15 minutes until lamb is tender. Stir in lemon or lime juice, season to taste. Serve with Basmati rice.

IRISH STEW

Gigot lamb chops or lamb pieces
onions, potatoes
carrots, fresh parsley
beef stock

Slice the onions into rings, cut peeled potatoes into thick chunks, slice carrots. Arrange meat, onions, carrots and the half the potatoes in layers in a saucepan, add chopped parsley and season liberally. Add stock and bring to the boil. Simmer 30 minutes, add remaining potatoes and cook until soft.

Fruity Lamb Kebabs

2lb(900g) lean lamb, cut in 1"(2.5cm) cubes
1 large red pepper, de seeded and cut in cubes
5oz(150g) no-soak dried apricots

MARINADE

1"(2.5cm) root ginger, peeled and chopped
1tbsp redcurrant jelly
1tsp wholegrain mustard
1tbsp tomato paste, 1tbsp fresh rosemary
2tbsp oil, salt and pepper

Beat the marinade ingredients together, stir in lamb and marinade for 4 hours. Drain the meat and thread onto 6 skewers alternately with red pepper and apricots. Grill kebabs under a medium heat for 10 minutes, turning occasionally. Serve on a bed of rice and a green salad.

Leaf Parcels

4oz(100g) smoked streaky bacon, de-rinded and chopped
1lb(450g) cooked lamb or pork finely minced
1oz(25g) butter, 1tbsp oil
1 clove garlic, peeled and crushed
1 large onion, chopped, 3oz(75g) cooked rice
1 egg, lightly beaten
1tbsp soy sauce
1tsp dried oregano, salt and black pepper
20 large Chinese lettuce leaves
1/4pt(150ml) boiling water

Oven 350°F/180°C/Gas4.
Cook garlic in hot fat for 1 minute. Add onion and cook until soft. Add bacon and cook for 2-3 minutes. Place in a electric mixer with minced meat, cooked rice, egg, soy sauce and oregano. Season generously. Mix until the ingredients are well combined. (This mixing can also be done with a wooden spoon or by hand). Pour boiling water into a large bowl, add Chinese leaves in two or three batches. Leave for a minute until softened. Remove leaves with a slotted spoon and plunge into cold water. Drain and pat dry with kitchen paper. Spread leaves out individually and using a sharp knife, cut away the thick spine in a `V' shape and discard. Take 1tbsp of meat filling and place in the centre of one of the leaves, Roll up the trimmed end of the leaf over the filling. Tuck in the sides to make sure the filling is securely enclosed. Repeat with other leaves. Pack the rolls tightly into a roasting tin. Pour over the stock and bake uncovered for 25 minutes until golden. Tip off the juices. Serve with tomato sauce. If Chinese leaves are not available substitute Savoy cabbage leaves.

* For spicy leaf parcels add 2 tsp of chili sauce (or to taste). Serve with a small bowl of sweet dipping chili sauce for each person

GREEK LAMB BAKE

1 onion, chopped
1lb(450g) minced lamb
2tbsp flour
1 clove garlic, crushed
1tbsp mint sauce
1tsp ground allspice
14oz(395g) can chopped tomatoes
2tbsp tomato puree
1/4pt(150ml) lamb or beef stock
8oz(225g) dried macaroni
salt and black pepper
1/4pt(150ml) Greek-style yoghurt
2 eggs, beaten
pinch grated nutmeg

Oven 350°F/180°C/Gas 4.
Stir fry the mince and onion until meat is browned. Stir in flour, garlic, mint sauce and allspice, stirring for 1 minute. Add tomatoes, puree and stock. Bring to the boil and simmer for 20 minutes, stirring occasionally. Cook the macaroni in boiling salted water for 8-10 minutes, until tender. Drain the pasta and stir into the mince mixture. Season to taste. Spoon into a large casserole dish. Beat the yoghurt and eggs together with nutmeg and seasoning. Pour over the macaroni mixture. Bake for 35-40 minutes until topping is set and golden brown. Serve hot or warm with a crisp salad.

* This mix can be used for a lasagne. Instead of macaroni use lasagne strips that don't need pre-cooking. Layer the mix and pasta into a casserole dish finishing with a layer of mixture. Optionally, layer slices of cheese on top before baking

LIVER & BACON HOTPOT

1lb(450g) lamb's liver, cut into 16 slices
1oz(25g) butter, 1tbsp oil
2 medium onions, sliced in rings
4 bacon rashers, rinds removed
1 cooking apple, peeled, cored and sliced
salt and black pepper, 2tsp Worcestershire sauce
1/2pt(300ml) hot beef stock, 1tsp cornflour

Oven 350°F/180°C/Gas 4.
Wash the liver and dry thoroughly. Heat the oil/butter in a large frying pan. Fry the liver slices until brown on both sides. Transfer to a plate. Lower heat and fry onion rings until soft. Spread the onions evenly over the base of a greased casserole dish. Make 8 `sandwiches' of half a rasher between two apple slices and two liver slices. Turn the `sandwiches' on their sides and arrange in a row on top of the onions. Season. Add Worcestershire sauce to the stock, stir in blended cornflour. Bring to the boil, stir until thickened. Pour over the liver. Cover and bake for 30 minutes. Serve hot.

CUTS OF PORK

Leg - this is a prime joint. It is usually cut in two pieces, knuckle and fillet or best end of leg. Both joints are ideal for roasting.

The knuckle end can be boned and stuffed. Slices cut from boned fillet can be grilled or fried.

Belly - usually boned and rolled for roasting. Thick slices of belly can be grilled, fried or used for stewing or braising. Sometimes this joint is salted in brine, boned, boiled and pressed for serving cold. Chinese spare ribs are cut from this joint.

Loin - divided into chump, middle and best or rib end of loin. The chump and middle loin can be roasted whole or cut into chops which can be fried, grilled or baked. Best rib end chops are best for grilling or frying.

Porksteak or Fillet - this is a lean thin piece of meat cut from the inside of the middle loin bone. It can be sliced for grilling, frying or flattened out for escalopes. The whole piece can be stuffed and roasted.

Shoulder - this large roasting joint can be boned and stuffed. Otherwise it is divided into smaller joints, spare rib, blade bone and hand and spring. These joints are all used for roasting on the bone or boned and stuffed. The spare rib joint can also be cut into chops for braising, frying or grilling.

Hand and Spring - this joint is also used for pies, stews and casseroles. It is this joint that will be used by the butcher for mince or pork pieces.

Spare Ribs - Chop into separate ribs. Coat with Hoisin sauce and bake covered in a hot oven for 20 minutes. Remove cover and bake for a further 10-15 minutes until well browned. Spare ribs can be baked without the coating sauce and then served with sweet and sour or barbecue sauce.

COOK'S TIPS

Baste roast pork with apple cider or pineapple juice for a lovely flavour.

Guarantee good crackling on your pork without over-cooking by rubbing salt well into the scored skin (cuts close together). Leave overnight, wipe off and rub the skin with cooking oil before putting into the oven.

PORK & BACON

ESCALOPES OF PORK

12oz(700g) porksteak or fillet
1tbsp flour, salt and black pepper
1 egg, lightly beaten
4oz(125g) fresh bread crumbs
herb pepper, mixed herbs, onion and garlic salt
1oz(25g) butter, 1tbsp oil
sliced gherkins, lemon wedges , sprigs parsley

Season the breadcrumbs with herbs, salt and pepper. Cut porksteak in half lengthways. Place between sheets of greaseproof paper or clingfilm. Beat gently with a rolling pin to flatten. Cut each piece into 4 escalopes. Coat each escalope with seasoned flour, beaten egg and bread crumbs, press crumbs on firmly. Heat oil and butter in a large frying pan. Fry escalopes for 5 minutes on each side. Drain on kitchen paper. Serve the escalopes garnished with sliced gherkins, lemon wedges and parsley.

* Alternative seasoning — Mix breadcrumbs with 1oz sesame seeds, salt and pepper and moisten with 3tsp soy sauce

PORK BALLOTINES

6 x 4oz(100g) porksteaks or fillet
1 bunch spring onions, 1 red pepper
2oz(50g) butter, 1tbsp oil
2oz(50g) fresh bread crumbs
3oz(75g) cream cheese with garlic and herbs
1/3pt(200ml) white wine

Oven 375°F/190°C/Gas5.
Put each porksteak between two sheets greaseproof paper and flatten with a rolling pin into a rectangle escalope. Chop spring onion, core,de-seed and chop pepper. Melt half the butter and oil in a pan, fry onion and pepper for two minutes until soft. Stir in breadcrumbs and fry for one minute. Cut the cream cheese into pieces and mix into the pepper mixture. Season. Spread over the escalopes and roll up from the short side. Secure with string at 1/2"(1cm) intervals. Place the 6 ballontines in a dish and cover with cling film, chill until required. Melt the remaining butter and oil in pan. Fry ballotines on all sides until golden. Transfer to a shallow ovenproof dish so that they fit closely together. Add wine to the pan and bring to the boil, stirring to remove all the sediment. Pour over the pork. Cover the dish tightly and cook for 30 minutes. Remove string before serving. Serves 6

ANOTHER FILLING FOR BALLOTINES

2oz(50g) prunes, stoned
3oz (75g) fresh white breadcrumbs
2oz(50g) soft cream cheese
2oz(50g) button mushrooms, chopped
1tbsp fresh parsley, 1 egg, size 3
juice of 1 lemon or orange

Combine the prunes, breadcrumbs, cheese, mushrooms, parsley and egg in a food processor for 40 seconds until smooth. Divide the stuffing between the escalopes. Secure with cocktail sticks or string. Place in roasting tin and pour the lemon or orange juice over them. Season with black pepper. Cook for 20- 25 minutes.

PORK CHOPS WITH ORANGE SAUCE

Pork chops or pieces of pork2
medium onions
1/2pt(300ml) orange juice, 2tbsp vinegar
1tbsp brown/white sugar
1tsp minced garlic (optional), salt and pepper
oil for frying

Toss the meat in seasoned flour and fry in a little oil until browned. Remove from pan and add sliced onions and garlic if used - cook until soft. Return meat to pan and add orange juice, vinegar and sugar. Cover and simmer for 30 minutes or until meat is tender. Serve with boiled potatoes, green vegetables and slices of orange.

* Alternatively rub the chops with garlic and oil and cook under the grill until browned. Continue with the recipe. Serve with rice instead of potatoes

PORK PROVENCALE

1oz(25g) butter, 1tbsp oil
1 large onion, sliced, 3 sticks celery, chopped
1/2 cucumber, diced, 14oz(400g) can chopped tomatoes
1/2tsp mixed herbs, 1/2tsp sugar.
salt and black pepper
4 pork chops
sprigs of parsley

Oven 375°F/190°C/Gas 5.
Fry onion and celery in hot oil/butter until soft. Stir in cucumber, tomatoes, herbs, sugar and seasoning. Bring to the boil and put into a shallow ovenproof dish. Lay the chops on top of the tomato mixture. Cook for 50 minutes until chops are tender. Garnish with parsley.

* To make even more Mediterranean, add 4oz olives (preferably stoned), 1oz capers and a red pepper to the vegetable mixture

SPICED PORK

2lb(900g) pork pieces
3tbsp oil
8oz(225g) onions, chopped
1 clove garlic, crushed
1tsp sugar
1 small chilli, seeded and chopped
1tbsp ground coriander
1/2tsp turmeric
1-2tsp hot curry paste
3/4pt(425ml) chicken stock
1/2pt(300ml) white wine
8oz(225g) pineapple
salt and pepper
2tbsp fresh coriander

Heat oil in a pan, brown the pork in small batches, remove from the pan and drain on kitchen paper. Add onion, garlic and sugar, add more oil if required, fry for 5 minutes. Stir in chilli, coriander and turmeric, fry for 1 minute. Add the chicken stock and wine. Bring to the boil, simmer 10 minutes. Add meat, pineapple and seasoning. Simmer 25-30 minutes until meat is tender. Stir in chopped coriander. Serve with a sprinkling of curried cashew nuts.

CURRIED CASHEW NUTS

1tbsp oil, 4oz(100g) unsalted cashew nuts
1tsp mild curry powder, salt and pepper

Heat the oil, cook the nuts, curry powder and seasoning for 3-4 minutes until lightly browned. Cool completely.

PORC A LA CREME

11/2lb(700g) pork fillet or pork pieces
1oz(25g) butter, 1tbsp oil
1 onion, peeled and chopped
1tbsp paprika pepper, 1tbsp flour
1/2pt(300ml) chicken stock, 5tbsp sherry, 2tsp tomato puree
6oz(175g) button mushrooms, salt and pepper
1tbsp cornflour, 1/4pt(150ml) fresh cream
sprigs parsley

Cut pork into 1"(2.5cm) cubes. Fry pieces in hot oil/butter until beginning to brown evenly. Remove and drain on kitchen paper. Fry onion and paprika for 2 minutes, add flour and cook for one minute. Remove from heat and add stock, sherry and tomato puree, return to heat, bring to boil, stirring until thick. Season and add meat. Cover and simmer for 30 minutes. Add mushrooms and cook for a few minutes. Add cornflour blended with a little water. Reheat and before serving stir in cream. Garnish with sprigs of parsley.

SWEET & SOUR PORK

8-10oz(225-275g) pork pieces
oil for frying
1/2pt(300ml) chicken stock, small tin pineapple pieces
2tsp brown sugar, 2tsp tomato ketchup
1tbsp cornflour, 1tbsp vinegar
1 carrot cut in strips
2tsp soy sauce, 2tsp lemon juice, 1 small garlic clove

Marinade the pork pieces in the soy sauce, lemon juice, crushed garlic and 4tbsp of pineapple juice, for a few hours or overnight. Drain pork pieces from the marinade and brown in hot oil. Add marinade and stock, simmer for 30 minutes. Drain remaining juice from pineapple, and put into a pan, blend in rest of ingredients except carrot. Add cooking stock and bring sauce to boil stirring all the time. Add pork pieces, pineapple and carrot. Simmer for 5-10 minutes. Serve with boiled rice or chips.

To make a greater contrast — add 3tsp chili sauce to the marinade and serve with a small bowl of sweet chili dipping sauce

CRISPY PORK WITH APPLE SAUCE

2lb(900g) belly of pork
4oz(225g) golden bread crumbs
grated rind 1 lemon, 1tbsp mustard powder
salt and black pepper, 1 egg, beaten

SAUCE

1lb(450g) cooking apples
1tbsp lemon juice, 2-3tbsp water
1oz(25g) butter, 1 small onion, chopped
sugar to taste

Oven 375°F/190°C/Gas 5.
Remove rind, bones and excess fat from the pork. Cut into 1/2inch strips. Mix the breadcrumbs with lemon rind, mustard and seasoning. Spread the mixture out on a large flat plate or a sheet of greaseproof paper. Dip each pork slice in beaten egg, allowing the surplus to drip off. Coat well with breadcrumbs. Arrange in a single layer in a greased, ovenproof dish or roasting tin. Bake for 40-50 minutes until cooked through and crisp on the outside. Make apple sauce - Place sliced apples in a saucepan with lemon juice and water. Simmer gently until soft. Melt butter in a pan, add onion and fry gently until golden brown. Add the onion to the cooked apple, sweeten to taste with sugar. Drain the cooked pork slices on absorbent paper and arrange on a serving dish and serve with apple sauce.

Spice the sauce with a little grated nutmeg and 2tsp mixed spice and add 4oz sultanas to the cooked apple mix

BRAISED PORK

3lb(1500g) blade of pork boned
1oz(25g) butter, 1tbsp oil
4 onions, sliced, 1tbsp flour
1/4pt(15ml) cider, 1/4pt(150ml) water
1/2tsp sugar, 1/4tsp dried sage,
salt and black pepper

Oven 350°F/180°C/Gas 4.
Cut off rinds and excess fat from meat. Roll up tightly and tie securely with string. Brown the meat on all sides in hot oil and butter. Place the meat in a large casserole. Add onions to hot fat and fry until soft, stir in flour, cider, water, sugar, sage and seasoning. Bring to the boil, stirring. Add to casserole. Cover and cook for 2 hours, until meat is tender. Take from the oven, remove string. Rest for a few minutes before carving.

PORK EN CROUTE

2lb(900g) lean minced pork
1 onion, finely chopped, 1 clove garlic, crushed
1tbsp chopped parsley
3 eggs
1tsp Worcestershire sauce
few drops Tabasco
4oz(100g) Gouda cheese, diced
6oz(150g) button mushrooms, chopped
1/4pt(150ml) chicken stock
8oz(225g) puff pastry

Oven 375°F/190°C/Gas 5.
Put the onion, garlic, parsley and two beaten eggs into a large bowl. Add seasoning, Worcestershire sauce (or 2tbsp tomato ketchup) and tabasco. Mix in the minced pork. Put half the mixture in greased 2lb(1.2ltr) loaf tin. Sprinkle cheese and mushrooms over the pork. Cover with remaining mixture, levelling the top firmly. Cover with foil and place in a roasting tin containing an 1"(5cm) of boiling water. Cook for an hour until browned and slightly shrunken from the sides of the tin. Pour off all the meat juices into a bowl containing the chicken stock. Turn out the loaf and weigh down under a board. Leave until cool. Roll out the puff pastry into an oblong large enough to completely enclose the loaf. Place on a greased baking tray with the join side downwards. Brush with remaining beaten egg. Make a few slashes on top to allow steam to escape. Bake at 450°F/225°C/Gas 8 for 20-25 minutes until pastry is crisp and golden. Serve with thickened stock. Serves 6

PORK WITH BLACK PUDDING

2 eating apples, peeled, cored and sliced
1/2pt(300ml) apple juice
2 pork fillets, 14oz(400g) each
4oz(100g) black pudding, mashed
salt and black pepper, 2tbsp olive oil
1 onion, peeled, chopped, 1 clove garlic, crushed
1/2pt(300ml) chicken stock
2tbsp creme fraiche

Put apple into a pan with 1/4pt(150ml) apple juice. Heat until softened. Slice into side of the escalope and open out, place between two sheets of clingfilm and beat to flatten. Spread the black pudding over the meat and put apple along the centre. Reserve the apple juice. Season and roll up the fillets, secure with cocktail sticks. Heat a little oil and sear the fillets on all sides over a high heat, reduce heat, cover the pan and cook for 20 minutes. Remove the pork from the pan and keep warm. Add the onion and garlic and cook for a few minutes, add remaining apple juice with stock, simmer and reduce sauce by half. Sieve into a clean pan, reheat and whisk in the creme fraiche, season to taste.

* Omit the black pudding and substitute with streaky bacon rashers

PORK & VEGETABLE LAYER

1lb(450g) lean minced pork
7fl oz(200ml) stock, 14oz(397g) can chopped tomatoes
1 chopped onion, 2oz(50g) sultanas, 2tbsp tomato puree
2tbsp chopped parsley, 2tsp chopped thyme
1tbsp Worcestershire Sauce, salt and black pepper
11/2lb(700g) potatoes, 8oz(225g) carrots
8oz(225g) courgettes
1/2pt(300ml) milk, 4tbsp cornflour, 4oz(100g) grated cheese
1/4tsp ground mace, 1/4tsp mustard powder

Oven 400°F/200°C/Gas 6.
Stir-fry the pork in a pan without adding any fat, for 8 minutes. Add the stock, tomatoes, onion, sultanas, tomato puree, Worcestershire sauce, herbs and seasoning. Cover and simmer for 20 minutes. Slice potatoes and carrots. Cook together in a pan of salted water for 8 minutes, drain. Blend 2tbsp cornflour with a little milk, add to remaining milk, heat, stirring until thickened. Add cheese, spices and seasoning. Blend the remaining 2tbsp cornflour with water and add to the meat sauce, cook for 2 minutes. Spoon meat into a greased, ovenproof dish, top with potatoes, carrots and sliced courgettes. Pour the cheese sauce over the top. Bake for 40 minutes. Serve garnished with parsley and quartered tomatoes. (Cheese sauce could also be made with flour and butter roux)

ROAST BELLY OF PORK

4lb(2kg) belly of pork boned
3oz(75g) crustless white bread, 6 large parsley sprigs,
2oz(50g) pitted prunes, 1 small onion, 1 dessert apple
1tbsp lemon juice, salt and pepper

Oven 425°F/220°C/Gas 7.
Make a cavity for the stuffing from where the bones were removed. Place the bread, prunes and parsley in the processor and chop finely. Add the grated onion and apple with the lemon juice and seasoning. Stuff the joint and secure with string. Sprinkle the skin with salt and roast skin side up for 20 minutes. Reduce the heat to 350oF/180oC/Gas 4 and cook for a further 2 hours until tender.

VEAL CASSEROLE WITH CREAM

11/2lb(750g) veal, cut into large cubes
2oz(50g) butter, 1tbsp oil
1 onion, 1 stalk celery, 4oz(125g) mushrooms
1/4pt(150ml) chicken stock, 1tsp paprika,
1/2tsp mixed herbs
2tbsp dry sherry or lemon juice, 1tsp salt, black pepper
1/4pt(150ml)fresh cream

Fry cubes of veal until lightly browned. Chop onion and celery, add with sliced mushrooms, cook until soft. Add stock, paprika, herbs, lemon juice or sherry and seasoning. Cover dish and cook for 1 hour until veal is tender. Stir in cream. Serves 4

VEAL ESCALOPES

4 slices veal, 2oz butter, 1tbsp oil
dry breadcrumbs, beaten egg
herb pepper, black pepper, garlic and onion salt
mixed herbs, parsley, tin anchovies

Beat each piece of veal until very thin. Add the seasoning to the breadcrumbs. Dip each escalope in the beaten egg and then in the seasoned breadcrumbs. Heat the butter and oil until very hot, fry each escalope for two minutes each side. Serve with mushroom cream sauce and drained anchovies that have been soaked in milk to remove saltiness.

BACON & POTATO CASSEROLE

Leftover bacon or ham, cooked potatoes
1pt(600ml) white sauce with onion and parsley added

Oven 375°F/190°C/Gas 5.
Put a layer of sliced potatoes in a wide, greased oven-proof dish. Make up three-quarters pint white sauce and add a chopped onion and a little fresh or dried parsley. Spoon over the potatoes. Scatter chopped chunks of cooked ham or gammon slices on top, cover with another layer of potatoes. Brush with a little melted butter or milk. Bake for 40 minutes.

SIZZLING HAM

8 slices cooked ham, 6oz(150g) button mushrooms
1/3pt(200ml) dry white wine
1 onion, finely chopped, 1lb(450g) tomatoes
1oz(50g) butter, 1tbsp oil, 1oz(25g) flour
1/2pt(300ml) milk, 4tbsp whipped fresh cream
2oz(50g) cheese, grated, salt and pepper

Oven 400°F/200°C/ Gas 6.
Roll up the ham slices and arrange in a greased ovenproof dish. Place the wine and thickly sliced mushrooms in a small pan and cook briskly until the wine is reduced to about 3tbsp. Remove the mushrooms and scatter over the ham rolls. Add onion to wine and cook until all the wine has evaporated. In another pan, melt butter/oil, add flour and gradually the milk. Stir until thickened, season well. Add cooked onion and cream. Skin the tomatoes, remove seeds and chop flesh. Add to the sauce. Pour over the ham and mushrooms. Top with grated cheese. Bake for 10 minutes until cheese has melted. Put under a hot grill for a few minutes to brown top. Serve immediately.

BACON STUFFED COURGETTES

6 courgettes, 1oz(25g) butter, 1tbsp oil
1 onion, peeled, chopped
12oz(350g) collar bacon, soaked
3 large tomatoes, peeled and chopped
1/2tsp mixed herbs or basil, salt and pepper

Oven 350°F/180°C/Gas 4.
Cut a deep wedge from each courgette, place in a greased casserole dish. Melt the butter/oil in a pan and fry the onion until soft. Mince the bacon and add to the pan. Stir-fry for 10 minutes. Add tomatoes, herbs and seasoning and spoon into courgettes. Cover with foil and cook in oven for 45 minutes. Serve hot. Vegetable marrow could also be used for this recipe. Remove a slice from the top and scoop out seeds. Fill with stuffing, top with lid, brush with melted butter and bake for 1 hour.

BAKED GAMMON

5lb(900g) piece of gammon
2tbsp soft brown sugar, 1tsp dry mustard, pepper
bunch spring onions
1/4pt(150ml) apple juice or cider, 2 cooking apples
1/4tsp ground cloves, 1oz(25g) butter

Oven 400°F/200°C/Gas 6.
Steep the piece of gammon for a few hours or overnight. Rinse under the cold tap and dry well. Combine 1tbsp sugar, mustard and pepper. Rub into sides of the piece of gammon. Place the gammon in a large, shallow casserole dish. Scatter the chopped spring onion over, and pour in the apple juice or cider. Cover tightly and bake for 30 minutes. Turn the gammon over and bake for a further 30 minutes. Turn gammon again, add cloves and cover with slices of peeled, cored apples. Sprinkle evenly with remaining sugar. Dot with pieces of butter, cover dish. Reduce oven to 350oF/180oC/Gas 4 and bake for 45 minutes until gammon is tender. Remove cover and cook a further 15 minutes. Allow to stand for 20 minutes in a warm place before slicing. Serves 6.

CUMBERLAND SAUCE

1 orange and 1 lemon
6tbsp redcurrant jelly, 6tbsp ruby port
1/2tsp Dijon mustard, 1/2tsp ground ginger
juice of half a lemon, juice of whole orange
salt and pepper

Pare the rind thinly from the orange and lemon, cut in very fine trips. Cook the strips in water for 5 minutes until tender. Drain and reserve strips. Heat the jelly and port until dissolved. Mix together the mustard, ginger, orange and lemon juice. Add to the melted jelly with the orange and lemon strips. Taste and season.

COOK'S TIPS

To make a quick white sauce, put the required amount of milk, flour and butter into a saucepan over a medium heat. Whisk constantly until it comes to the boil and thickens. Season to taste.

To cook vegetables grown underground, place in cold water. Vegetables grown above ground should be put into boiling water. Leave greens uncovered during cooking.

Add a small knob of butter to the water of boiling vegetables to stop them boiling over.

To prevent an unpleasant odour when cooking cabbage, add a slice of raw apple or a few bay leaves to the water.

To keep a head of cabbage fresh, hollow out the pith in the stalk. Fill the hollow with fresh water every day and store the cabbage upside down.

To scrape carrots quickly, immerse them in hot water for a few seconds and the skin will come off easily.

To keep celery fresh, trim and wash it. Cut off the neck from a 2 litre drinks bottle to make a tall container. Add a cupful of water and stand the stalks in it. Renew the water daily.

To keep cauliflower fresh, cut off all the green leaves, wrap tightly with clingfilm and stand on its florets in the refrigerator.

Add a few sprigs of parsley to broad beans when cooking to give a good colour and improve the flavour.

If you want to peel potatoes hours before use, add a few drops of vinegar to the water they are soaking in or put a slice of white bread on top.

For roasted potatoes or parsnips, first cover with hot water and bring to the boil. Drain and toss in oil before placing in the oven.

To easily skin pickling onions, plunge them quickly into hot water (just off the boil), then into cold water before skinning. Vegetables like mange tout or snap peas should be brought to the boil in salted water and drained (reserve water). Refresh under cold running water to retain their bright green colour. Reheat in reserved water, drain and serve.

VEGETABLES

POTATO, CARROT & ONION BORGUIGNONNE

8oz(225g) carrots, 8oz(225g) potatoes, sliced
8oz(225g) small onions
4oz(125g) button mushrooms
1oz(25g) butter, 1tbsp oil
1oz(25g) syrup, 1tbsp flour
1/4pt(150ml) red wine, 1/4pt(150ml) beef stock
2tsp tomato puree
1 bay leaf, salt and black pepper

Heat the oil and butter, add syrup, carrots, onions and potatoes. Cook until brown. Add mushrooms and cook a further minute. Stir in flour, scraping all the sediment from the pan. Add the remaining ingredients, stir, cover tightly and cook for 30 minutes or until tender. Remove bay leaf before serving. Garnish with chopped parsley.

* This can be topped with a layer of sliced potatoes, seasoned and overlaid with a covering of cheddar cheese for a filling meal on its own

SCALLOPED POTATOES

1 1/2lb(700g) potatoes, sliced thinly
1 onion, grated or finely chopped
1 clove garlic, crushed
1/2pt(300ml) milk, 1/2 vegetable stock cube
salt and pepper, a little cream

Oven 350°F/180°C/Gas 4.
Place the sliced potatoes in a greased shallow oven-proof dish layered with onion, garlic and seasoning. Cover completely with milk and leave to stand for a few hours. Melt the stock cube in a little hot milk and pour over the dish. Bake for an hour until potatoes are soft and topping is golden. Pour a little cream over the top and sprinkle with chopped parsley.

* For variation, grated cheese can be layered with the potatoes.

* Alternatively chop a generous handful of parsley into the mixture

SAUTE POTATOES

1lb(450g) potatoes,
1oz(25g) butter, 1tbsp oil, 1 clove garlic crushed
mixed herbs, onion salt, paprika, salt and pepper

Boil the potatoes in their jackets until they are almost tender. Drain and leave to cool. Peel the potatoes and cut into large dice. Melt the butter and oil in a hot frying pan and add the potato dice. Sprinkle over the herbs, garlic and seasoning. When browned on the bottom, turn the potatoes and cook until golden. Drain on kitchen paper before serving.

* *When the potatoes are almost browned toss a handful of sesame seeds into the fan to flash fry with the potatoes. A few dill seeds as well will add a touch of aniseed flavour*

ROASTED POTATO & PARSNIP

Place a roasting tin with 2oz(50g) fat in a hot oven. Peel potatoes and cut in half, if large. Peel parsnips and cut into long `chips'. Put both vegetables into a pan of hot, salted water, bring to the boil and cook for 4 minutes. Drain, cool and pat dry. Coat in oil and place in the hot tin, bake for 30 minutes turning occasionally.

* *Scattering a generous amount of sunflower seeds over the vegetables before baking to give extra crunch*

BUBBLE & SQUEAK BAKE

2lb(1kg) potatoes, peeled, knob of butter and a little milk
salt and black pepper
1lb(450g) firm green cabbage, 1 medium onion, chopped
2 medium carrots, grated
6oz(175g) Cheddar cheese grated

Oven 400°F/200°C/Gas 6.
Cook the potatoes in boiling salted water until tender. Drain, season and cream with butter and milk. Slice the cabbage, cook and drain well, reserving the water. Chop the cabbage. Put onion and carrot into the cabbage water and cook for 5 minutes. Drain. Mix the cabbage and potato together, spread half of the mixture in a buttered ovenproof dish, then the onion and carrot. Sprinkle 4oz(125g) cheese over the top. Cover with the rest of the cabbage and potato mixture. Smooth the surface, score with a fork and mark into portions. Sprinkle the remaining cheese on top. Bake for 40 minutes until golden.

* *This dish can be made with a number of different vegetables including broccoli, spinach, celery, parsnips, small turnips*

CREAMED CABBAGE

1 head green cabbage, 1/2 small onion, grated
1/4pt(150ml) creamy white sauce, salt and pepper

Remove the dark green leaves from the cabbage and wash well. Shred, removing any hard cores. place in a pan of hot salted water (cooking water from ham or bacon is ideal). Cook for 15 minutes, then add the shredded white cabbage. Cook a further five minutes and drain well in a colander. Return the cabbage to the pan, add grated onion and enough white sauce to coat the cabbage. Season to taste. Serve hot.

* Add chopped parsley to the white sauce or omit the sauce altogether and just stir in plenty of salted butter to coat the cabbage

BAKED CABBAGE WITH CREAM

1lb(450g) cabbage, 1/4pt(150ml) fresh single cream
1tsp caster sugar, 1/2tsp salt, 1/2tsp paprika
4tbsp toasted bread crumbs, 3oz(75) grated cheese

Oven 325°F/170°C/Gas3.
Shred the cabbage finely, put into a buttered dish. Combine the cream with sugar, salt and paprika, pour over the cabbage. Sprinkle bread- crumbs on top. Cover dish and bake for 30 minutes. Remove from oven, sprinkle with cheese and brown under the grill.

* Instead of cream use plain yogurt or fromage frais

RED CABBAGE

1oz(25g) butter, 1tbsp oil
1 onion, thinly sliced, 1 clove garlic, crushed
1/2 head red cabbage, finely shredded
1 large cooking apple, chopped, 1/2tsp mixed spice
3tbsp water, 2-3tbsp wine vinegar, 3tbsp red wine
2tbsp brown sugar, salt and pepper

Melt the butter and oil and fry the onion and garlic until soft but not brown. Add the cabbage, apple, spice, water, vinegar and wine, Cover the pan with a tight fitting lid. Cook for 35-40 minutes until the cabbage is tender. Add sugar and seasoning to taste.

* This dish can also be baked in a covered casserole dish in a medium oven. Stir from time to time

RED CABBAGE PARCELS

4 large red cabbage leaves
1lb(450g) broccoli florets
5oz(150g) cream cheese, 1tbsp low-fat natural yoghurt
1oz(25g) pine kernels
1/2pt(300)ml white wine
dill sprigs and curly endives to garnish
1/4pt(150ml) fromage frais, 2tbsp freshly chopped dill

Wash the red cabbage leaves and plunge them into boiling salted water for 2 minutes, drain well. Cook the broccoli in boiling salted water for 7 minutes, drain well. Cut into small florets. Beat the cream cheese and yoghurt together until smooth. Place a layer of broccoli then a spoonful of cheese mixture sprinkled with pine nuts into each cabbage leaf. Fold over to completely encase the filling. Place in a flame proof dish, seam side down, pour over wine and poach gently for 5 minutes. Remove the parcels from the liquid. Serve with fromage frais mixed with dill.

* Alternative filling — instead of broccoli use tinned corn or fresh baby corn

BRAISED CHICORY & ONIONS

4 heads of chicory
2 oranges, peeled and segmented
1 bunch spring onions, trimmed
1/2pt(300ml) orange juice
2tsp arrowroot, 1tbsp honey

Oven 350°F/180°C/Gas 4.
Plunge the chicory into salted water for 10 minutes, drain. Place in an ovenproof dish with orange segments and juice. Slice all but 2 spring onions and add to chicory. Cover the dish and cook for 1 hour. Drain liquid into a pan, keep chicory warm. Blend arrowroot with a little water, stir into the liquid with honey. Cook on a low heat until thickened. Pour sauce over chicory, garnish with spring onion tassles.

* To make this into a filling meal on its own cover the finished dish before cooking with a layer of scalloped potatoes

ORANGE GLAZED ONIONS

10-12oz(275-350g) small onions, peeled and cut in quarters
1/2pt(300ml)stock
1tsp brown sugar, knob of butter
1tbsp orange juice, cornflour to thicken

Put the quartered onions in a pan and cover with stock. Bring to the boil and simmer 15-20 minutes, until the liquid has reduced by half. Add butter, sugar and orange juice and cook a further five minutes. Thicken sauce with a little cornflour.

* For a richer dish add a glass of red wine to the cooking stock and a spoonful of marmalade to the reduced liquid

GOLDEN CAULIFLOWER

1 cauliflower, 1lb(450g) potatoes, diced
1/2oz(15g) butter, 2tbsp oil
1tsp mustard seeds(optional)
1tsp turmeric, 1tbsp sesame seeds, salt and pepper

Heat the butter and oil in a pan. Add the potato and cauliflower, cut into florets. Cook for a few minutes. If using mustard seeds, crush them and add with turmeric, sesame seeds and seasoning. Stir well. Cover and cook gently for 10 minutes, shaking the pan occasionally.

* Omit the turmeric, mustard and salt and instead crumble a blue cheese with the sesame seeds and pepper into the dish

CURRIED CAULIFLOWER

1 cauliflower
2oz(50g) butter, 1tbsp oil
2 tomatoes, 1 large onion, chopped
1/2pt(300ml) chicken stock, 2tsp curry powder
2 hard-boiled eggs, chopped
cornflour(optional)

Cut the cauliflower into sprigs. Blanch for two minutes in boiling salted water and drain well. Heat the butter an oil and cook onion for a few minutes. Add tomato and cauliflower. Mix the rest of the ingredients, except the egg, and add to the pan. Cover and simmer gently for 10 minutes. Thicken the sauce with cornflour. Serve sprinkled with egg.

VEGETABLES

RATATOUILLE

1 large aubergine, sliced, 1 large onion, sliced
2 medium courgettes, sliced
1 medium green pepper, de-seeded and chopped
1 clove garlic, crushed
8oz(225g) skinned tomatoes or tinned plum tomatoes
1tbsp olive oil, 2tbsp sunflower oil
1/2tsp salt and black pepper
2tbsp finely chopped parsley, 2tsp oregano

Place slices of aubergine and courgette flat on a plate and sprinkle well with salt, leave for 15 minutes. Rinse and dry well. Fry onions and garlic in hot oils for 3-4 minutes. Add aubergine, courgettes, pepper, tomatoes, parsley, oregano and seasoning. Stir well. Cover pan and simmer gently without stirring for 40 minutes. Serve hot or cold

QUARTER BACKS

2 red and 2 yellow peppers
2tbsp olive oil
8 rashers bacon, 1 clove garlic, crushed
1 small red chilli, de-seeded and chopped
1tbsp capers, rinsed and chopped
8tbsp white breadcrumbs, salt and pepper

Oven 425°F/220°C/Gas7.
Quarter the peppers, remove the core and seeds. Brush them inside and out with olive oil, and put them in a roasting tin, cut side up. Lay the bacon rashers across the top of the peppers. Bake for 10-15 minutes until the bacon is crispy. Snip the bacon into small pieces, add to the rest of the ingredients except the peppers, but pour the juice from the roasting tin. Divide the stuffing between the peppers, drizzle with a little oil and bake for a further 15-20 minutes

SUNSHINE CARROTS

1lb(450g) small carrots, 1tbsp brown sugar
1tsp cornflour, 1/4tsp ginger, salt and pepper
1/4pt(150ml) fresh orange juice, 1oz(25g) butter
parsley

Cook the carrots in salted water until tender, drain. Combine the sugar, cornflour, ginger and seasoning in a small saucepan, blend in the orange juice, bring to the boil, stirring until the mixture thickens. Stir in the butter and pour over the carrots. Garnish with chopped parsley.

CARROT RING

1lb(450g) carrots, chopped, 1/2pt(300ml) stock
1/2tbsp caster sugar, 2oz(50g) butter, melted,
2oz(50g) grated cheese, 1 egg size 3
1/2tsp ground mace, salt and pepper

Oven 350°F/180°C/Gas 4.
Place the first four ingredients in pan. Cover and cook until carrots are tender and liquid absorbed. Mash carrots, combine with cheese, egg, mace and seasoning. Spoon into a ring mould. Bake for 40 minutes. To serve, invert onto a plate and fill the centre with cooked peas.

VEGETABLE LAYER

4 carrots, peeled, 3 medium potatoes
3oz(75g) butter, seasoning

Oven 400°F/200°C/Gas 6.
Using a potato peeler cut the carrots into thin strips. Slice the potatoes very thinly. Blanch the carrot strips and potato slices in a large pan of boiling water for 1 minute. Drain well. Brush a little of the melted butter around the sides and base of a small ovenproof dish. Arrange carrot and potato in layers in the dish, adding melted butter and seasoning every few layers. Press down well and cover with foil. Bake for 30 minutes. Turn onto an ovenproof plate, brush with any remaining butter and return to the oven and cook 10-15 minutes until golden.

SHAKEN PEAS

12oz(350g) frozen peas, 1/2 lettuce, finely shredded
1 clove garlic, crushed, 1 onion, finely sliced
1oz(25g) butter, 1/2tsp castor sugar
1tbsp cream, roux to thicken
salt and pepper, chopped mint

Melt butter, fry onion and garlic until soft. Add the peas and shake the pan until the juices start to draw (no water is required). Simmer for 2-3 minutes, add the lettuce, sugar and season lightly. Simmer a further 2 minutes. Add the cream. Thicken slightly with roux. Stir in chopped mint and serve immediately.

COURGETTES IN TOMATO SAUCE WITH CHEESE

2lb(900g) young courgettes
2lb(900g) tomatoes, skinned, de-seeded and sliced
1oz(25g) butter and 2tbsp olive oil
2 cloves garlic, crushed, 1tsp sugar
1tbsp chopped parsley, 6oz(175g) grated cheese
salt and pepper

Oven 425°F/220°C/Gas7.
Top, tail and remove some skin from courgettes. Cut into
1/4"(5mm) disks. Melt butter and oil and fry courgettes in
batches until golden brown. Add tomatoes, garlic, sugar and
parsley. Mix well and season. Transfer into a baking dish,
sprinkle with cheese. Bake until brown and bubbling.

COURGETTES WITH PEAS & HERBS

4 medium courgettes, cut into 1/4"(5mm) cubes
juice of half a lemon, 1oz(25g) butter
8oz(225g) small frozen peas, defrosted
1tbsp fresh basil or oregano (or 11/2tsp dried oregano)
1tsp castor sugar, salt and black pepper

Toss courgettes in lemon juice to stop discolouration. Melt
butter, add peas, courgettes and the rest of ingredients. Turn
and stir gently until piping hot and vegetables cooked but
crisp. Serve in the pan juices.

** For a hotter flavour add 2tsp (or to taste) chili sauce or a couple of drops of
Tabasco*

BROCCOLI PUREE IN TOMATO CUPS

1lb(450g) broccoli
4-5 beef tomatoes
1 egg
1-2tbsp mayonnaise or fresh cream
salt and freshly ground black pepper
pinch nutmeg, 1/2tsp French mustard

Oven 400°F/200°C/Gas6.
Cut the broccoli into florets, including some of the main stalk.
Steam until just tender. Cut the beef tomatoes in half, scoop
out the centre. Place the tomato cases in a lightly greased
ovenproof dish, trim a slice of the base to make steady. Puree
the cooked broccoli. Whisk together the egg and cream or
mayonnaise, add the broccoli puree. Season with salt, pepper,
nutmeg and mustard. spoon generously into the tomato cases.
Bake for 15-20 minutes until the tomato is tender and the
broccoli slightly browned.

Broccoli with Mushroom & Sherry Sauce

1lb(450g) broccoli, trimmed and washed
1/2oz(50g) butter
6oz(175g) mushrooms, wiped and finely chopped
1/2oz(12g) flour, 1/2pt(300ml) milk
salt and pepper, 1-2tbsp dry light sherry

Cook broccoli, slightly salted water until tender. Melt the butter and saute the mushrooms for 5 minutes. Add the flour and cook for 1 minute. Remove from the heat and add the milk, stirring well. Return to the heat and bring sauce to the boil until smooth and thick. Add sherry and cook a further minute. Drain broccoli and place in a warmed serving dish. Pour over the sauce and serve immediately.

Creamed Green Beans

1lb(450g) French green beans, 2oz(50g) sliced mushrooms
1oz(25g) butter, 1/4pt(150ml) cream

Top and tail the beans. Slice diagonally into thin strips. Cook in boiling salted water until tender. Fry mushrooms in butter. Drain beans and add to mushrooms with cream, mix well. Reheat gently.

* For creamed Broad Beans follow the recipe as above using 1lb(450g) broad beans. Broad beans can also be served with 1/2pt(300ml) of well seasoned white sauce.

Sweet & Sour Beetroot

2tsp cornflour, 3fl oz(90ml) water
1 lemon, grated rind and juice
2tbsp clear honey, 2tbsp soy sauce
2tbsp white wine vinegar
1lb(450g) cooked beetroot

Combine the first six ingredients. Bring to the boil, stirring continuously, until thickened. Add beetroot and cook for 2-3 minutes to heat through. Serve garnished with chives.

Beetroot in Orange Sauce

1 stock cube diluted in 1/2pt(300ml) water
1 small onion, finely sliced, 2tsp tomato puree
1 small clove garlic, crushed, 1/4tsp curry powder
juice of 2 oranges, grated rind of one orange
1oz(25g) butter, 1oz(25g) flour, salt and pepper

Melt butter, add onion and fry until soft, add flour, stock and orange juice. Bring to the boil, add puree, garlic, curry powder, orange rind and seasoning. simmer for 10 minutes, strain and serve poured over sliced cooked beetroot.

ALADS

SPICED SAVOURY RICE

1lb(450g) long grain rice
1 green pepper, de seeded, 2 tomatoes, de seeded
2tbsp raisins, 1 small onion
small tin pineapple, drained and juice reserved

SAUCE

1/2 cup oil, 3tbsp vinegar
1/2 lemon juice, 1tbsp pineapple juice
1 small clove garlic, crushed, 1tsp sugar, 1tsp curry powder
1/2tsp ginger, salt and pepper

Cook the rice until soft. Rinse in cold water and drain well. Chop peppers, tomatoes, onion and pineapple into small pieces. Add to the rice with raisins. Make sauce by combining all the ingredients together. Add to the rice mixture in spoonfuls, mixing well. All the sauce may not be required.

* Alternatively — combine 8oz(225g) cooked rice and 8oz(225g) grated cheddar cheese with chopped cucumber, tomato, raisins, and pineapple. Serve with a tangy dressing - mix a tablespoon of chopped chives and 1/2 lemon juice into a carton of natural yoghurt. Season to taste.

GRILLED PEPPER SALAD

3 red peppers and 3 yellow peppers, halved and de-seeded
2tsp chopped fresh oregano or basil
1 clove garlic, crushed, 1tbsp wine vinegar, 4tbsp olive oil

Rinse and dry the peppers, then grill them until the skin is blistered and slightly charred. Place in a plastic bag and close loosely. Leave until cool enough to handle, peel off the skin. Cut the peppers into thin strips. Place in a dish with herbs and seasoning. Mix the garlic with wine vinegar and olive oil, pour over the peppers. Cover and leave to stand for at least 24 hours.

* A Mediterranean touch — when ready to serve add a scattering of olives, 2tsp of capers and 6-8 sliced anchovy fillets

SALAD DRESSING

1/3 jar wine or cider vinegar, 2/3 jar vegetable oil
4tsp sugar, 2tsp Dijon mustard, salt and black pepper
1 clove garlic, crushed, chopped fresh (or dried) tarragon

Add all the ingredients to a cold sterilised jar and shake well.

* A few drops of balsamic vinegar will enrich the dressing

PASTA SALAD

8oz(225g) baby shell pasta, 2oz(50g) grated cheese
2oz(50g) cooked ham, chopped cucumber, diced small
2 tomatoes, de-seeded and chopped, 1 onion, chopped finely
2tbsp each mayonnaise and salad cream (or yoghurt)
salt and pepper

Cook pasta according to instructions on packet. Drain and rinse under a cold tap. Drain well and put into a large bowl with other ingredients - these can be varied depending on what is available. Mix equal amounts of mayonnaise and salad cream(or yoghurt) together and add to pasta.

POTATO SALAD

Freshly boiled potatoes in their jackets, salad dressing
Home-made mayonnaise, a little milk
spring onion, salt and freshly ground black pepper

Peel the potatoes when still warm. Cut into small chunks. Place in a bowl and sprinkle with a little salad dressing. Leave until cold. Add some chopped spring onion. Thin the mayonnaise with a little milk and combine with the potatoes. Season to taste with salt and black pepper.

CARROT SALAD

3 carrots, grated, 1tbsp cooking oil
1tbsp yellow mustard seeds, 1tbsp lemon juice
salt and freshly ground black pepper

Heat the oil in a pan, add the mustard seeds, cover the pan and heat until the seeds pop and turn black. Add the grated carrot and cook for a few minutes stirring constantly. Remove from the heat and add 1tbsp lemon juice and seasoning to taste. Cool completely before serving.

MAYONNAISE

3 egg yolks, 1tsp Dijon mustard, 1tsp sugar, 1pt(600ml) oil
1 clove garlic, crushed(optional), 2tbsp wine vinegar,
fresh or dried tarragon(optional), salt and white pepper

Whisk the egg yolks in the food processor until creamy, add mustard, seasoning, sugar, garlic and herbs if using. Process for a minute. With the motor running, drip in the oil until the mixture starts to emulsify, then you can add the oil in a thin steady trickle. When about half the oil is in, add the 1tbsp wine vinegar, then trickle in the remaining oil. Taste for seasoning and add the remaining vinegar to taste. If the mixture curdles - pour the curdled mixture into a jug, wash the processor bowl and whisk a fresh egg yolk until creamy, add the curdled mixture drop by drop until the mixture emulsifies again, then add any remaining oil. Store in a screw-top, cold, sterilised jar in the refrigerator, use within two weeks.

COOKS TIPS

To sterilise jars - wash in warm, soapy water, rinse thoroughly in warm water. Dry well with a clean towel. Place upside down in a moderate oven 350°F/180°C/Gas 4 for 5-10 minutes. Use warm or cold.

Fruit for jam making should be firm, under-ripe or only just ripe and fresh. Over-ripe fruit will be lacking in pectin or acid and cause setting problems. The fruit should be cleaned before use and as dry as possible.

Fruit in good condition may be frozen when in season. Defrost the fruit in pan over heat. Add 1/8 extra fruit to recipe quantity to make up for loss of pectin or add 2tbsp lemon juice.

Choose a good quality large saucepan with a heavy base.

To allow room for the jam to boil vigorously - the pan should be about half full when the sugar has been added. Scum should only be removed at the end of cooking. Rub a piece of butter over the bottom of the pan to help avoid scum and prevent sticking.

Only add the sugar when the fruit is well cooked and soft. Boil the jam briskly until setting point is reached.

To test for setting - remove the jam from the heat and pour a scant teaspoonful of the jam onto a cold saucer and leave for 1 minute. Setting point has been reached if the surface sets and crinkles when pushed with the finger. A sugar thermometer will register about 220°F/105°C once setting point has been reached.

$\mathscr{P}$RESERVES

LEMON CURD

4oz(100g) butter, 8oz(200g) granulated sugar
3 eggs plus 1 yolk (size 3), 3 medium-sized lemons

Melt the butter in a double saucepan (or a basin standing over a saucepan of gently simmering water). Beat the eggs and yolk together, add to the melted butter with the sugar and finely grated rind and juice of the lemons. Cook gently without boiling until the mixture thickens sufficiently to coat the back of a spoon. Do not overheat or the mixture may curdle and separate. Pour into sterilised jars* and cover. Store in a very cool place and use within 2 weeks. Makes 11/4lb(500g)

BLACKCURRANT JAM

2lb(1kg) stemmed and washed blackcurrants
11/2pts(900ml) water, 3lb(1.5kg)granulated sugar
1/2oz(15g) butter

Put the blackcurrants and water into a large saucepan and bring to the boil, cover pan and reduce heat. Simmer gently for about 40 minutes until the fruit is tender. Add the sugar, stir until dissolved. Bring to the boil and boil briskly for 5-10 minutes (until setting point is reached). Remove the pan from the heat and stir in the butter to disperse scum. Pot and cover. Makes about 5lb(2.5kg) jam.

GOOSEBERRY JAM

Follow the recipe and method for Blackcurrant Jam. Use gooseberries instead of blackcurrants and halve the quantity of water. Boil for 10-15 minutes (or until setting point is reached. Makes about 5lb(2.5kg) jam.

* For extra sweetness add a can of halved pineapple chunks

DAMSON JAM

Follow the recipe and method for Blackcurrant Jam. Use damsons instead of blackcurrants and halve the quantity of water. Boil for 10-15 minutes after adding sugar (or until setting point is reached. Remove the stones with a perforated spoon as they rise to the surface.Makes 5lb(2.5kg) jam.

* A few sliced almonds can be added to the cooked jam before bottling

PRESERVES

APPLE & BLACKBERRY JAM

12oz(375g) apples (after peeling and coring)
2lb(1kg) blackberries, 1/4pt(150ml) water
3lb(1.5kg) granulated sugar, 1/2oz(15g) butter

Slice the apples thinly and put into a saucepan with blackberries, add the water, bring to the boil, reduce the heat and simmer in covered pan for 10-15 minutes. Crush the fruit against the sides of the pan until it is soft and pulpy. Add the sugar, heat slowly, stirring continuously until the sugar dissolves. Bring to the boil and boil briskly for 10-15 minutes (or until setting point is reached). Remove from the heat, stir in the butter to disperse scum. Pot and cover. Makes 5lb(2.5kg) jam.

* Hedgerow blackberries and crab apples make the best jam but discard any mouldy blackberries. Crab apples provide a tarter flavour than dessert apples.

STRAWBERRY JAM

31/2lb(1.75kg) strawberries
juice 1 large lemon
3lb(1.5kg) granulated sugar
1/2oz(15g) butter

Put the strawberries, lemon juice and sugar into the pan. Heat slowly, stirring until the sugar dissolves. Bring to the boil and boil briskly for 10-15 minutes (or until setting point is reached). Remove from the heat, stir in butter to disperse scum. Leave jam to cool in pan until skin forms on the surface. Stir gently, pot and cover. Makes 5lb(2,5kg) jam.

* Wild strawberry jam is delicious but difficult to get enough strawberries. Reduce the quantities of other ingredients in proportion to the weight of fruit

CURRIED FRUIT CHUTNEY

8 large cooking apples, 2 onions
8oz(225g) raisins, 4oz(100g)sultanas
14oz(410g) tin peaches, 1 large red pepper
1pt(600ml vinegar
8oz(225g) sugar, 2tbsp malt extract
1tsp salt, 1tsp ground ginger
1tbsp hot curry powder

Peel core and slice the apples, chop onion finely, de-seed and chop pepper finely. Put the apples, onion, pepper and vinegar in a large pan and bring to the boil, cover and simmer 30 minutes until the apple is soft. Chop the peaches and add with the juice to the pan with remaining ingredients. Stir well to dissolve sugar. Bring to the boil and cook, uncovered, until the chutney is thick, 40-60 minutes. Spoon into warm sterilised jars and cover when cold.

APPLE CHUTNEY

4lb(1.8kg) cooking apples (when peeled and chopped)
2lb(900g) onions (when peeled and chopped)
1lb(450g) sultanas, 1lb(450g) brown sugar
1pt(600ml) malt vinegar
1tsp salt, 1tsp cinnamon, 1tsp ginger
1tsp ground cloves, 1/2tsp chilli powder

Put sliced apple, onion, sultanas, spices, salt and vinegar into a saucepan. Bring to the boil, simmer 30-40 minutes until apples are soft. Add sugar and stir until dissolved. Boil chutney until thick. Spoon into warm sterilised jars and cover when cool.

PICKLED CAULIFLOWER

Break the heads of sound white cauliflower into small pieces. Place in a large basin, cover with brine made from 1lb(450g) salt to 1 gallon (4.5ltr) water, and allow to stand for 24 hours. Drain thoroughly, pack into jars, cover with cold spiced vinegar and seal.

* For a sweeter pickle add a teaspoonful of sugar for each jar, but dissolve this in the vinegar a few days before the pickle is required.

SWEETCORN RELISH

1lb(450g) frozen sweetcorn, defrosted
1 green and 1 red pepper, de-seeded and diced
1 large onion, 1 clove garlic, 1tbsp corn oil
1tbsp cornflour, 1pt(600ml) white vinegar, 6oz(175g) sugar
1tsp turmeric, 2tsp mustard powder, 1tsp ground white pepper
1tsp salt

Mix the cornflour to a smooth cream with a little vinegar. Heat the oil in a pan and fry the finely chopped onion and crushed garlic until soft. Add peppers, vinegar, sweetcorn, granulated sugar, mustard and turmeric to the pan and heat gently, stirring until the sugar is dissolved, bring to the boil. Simmer for 10 minutes, remove from the heat and add the cornflour mix. Return to the heat and simmer for a further 10 minutes. Season with salt and pepper. Put into warm jars and cover immediately. Use when cold or store for up to six months.

BEETROOT PICKLE

Wash the beets, being careful not to break the skins, Place in boiling salted water and simmer gently for 11/2 hours . Allow to go cold, peel and slice into 1/4"(5mm) thick rounds. Pack into sterilised jars and cover with cold spiced vinegar. A teaspoonful of salt may be added to each pint of spiced vinegar, if liked.

MIXED PEPPER RELISH

2 red and 2 yellow peppers, de-seeded and cut into strips
4 cloves garlic, sliced
1pt(600ml) white wine vinegar
4tbsp caster sugar, 1tsp salt

Blanch the peppers in boiling water for 1 minute until softened. Drain and pack into warm, dry sterilised jars with the garlic. Put the vinegar, sugar and salt into a pan and stir over a gentle heat until the sugar dissolves. Bring to the boil, pour the hot liquid over the peppers. Add extra vinegar if the peppers are not completely covered. Leave a little space at the top of the jar to prevent the vinegar coming in contact with the lid. Leave to mature a week in the refrigerator before using.

* *For a hotter relish add a whole red chili pepper to the jar*

SPICED VINEGAR

2pt(1ltr) vinegar
small bay leaf
1tbsp mace, whole allspice and whole cloves
7"(18cm) cinnamon stick
6 peppercorns

Put all the ingredients into a saucepan and bring to the boil. Remove from the heat immediately and pour into a jar, cover and leave to infuse for 2 hours. Strain through muslin, pour into sterilised bottles with airtight, vinegar-proof tops. Alternatively, put the spices into cold vinegar and leave to stand for 1-2 months, strain and bottle as above.

* *This spiced vinegar can be used to pickle onions or for tarragon vinegar*

* *When pickling vegetables which should be kept crisp, use cold vinegar.*

* *For soft fruits such as plums or pears, use hot vinegar.*

* *Small silverskin onions can be added to the beetroot pickle. Peel and gently simmer the onions for 5 minutes. When cold, bottle with the beetroot*

CUCUMBER PICKLE

2 cucumbers
4oz(100g) onion, thinly sliced
6oz(175g) granulated sugar, 1/2tbsp salt
1/2pt(300ml) white wine vinegar

Using a potato peeler take lengthways strips of skin from the cucumber. Slice finely in the processor. Add the thinly sliced onion. Combine the sugar, salt and vinegar in a jug and stir well. Add to the cucumber and mix well. Leave in the refrigerator for at least 1 hour. Fill sterilised jars, covering the cucumber mixture totally with liquid. Seal tightly.

MARINADES

Marinades tenderise, moisten and flavour any meat or fish. Simply whisk ingredients in a non-metallic dish, add the food and cover. Leave for at least 1 hour and turn regularly. Food will marinate more quickly at room temperature but in warm weather it is safer to keep in the refrigerator. The following marinades are for 6-8 pieces of meat or fish.

MEAT

1/4pt(150ml) red wine, 3tbsp oil
1tsp mustard, 1 crushed garlic clove
2 crumbled, dried bay leaves, ground black pepper

LAMB OR OILY FISH

4fl oz(120ml) dry cider, 1tbsp olive oil
2tbsp chopped fresh rosemary
1tsp mustard, ground black pepper

CHICKEN OR WHITE FISH

4tbsp oil
grated rind and juice of 1 lemon
3tbsp chopped fresh herbs
ground black pepper

PORK OR CHICKEN

3tbsp each of Hoisin sauce, soy sauce, dry sherry
2tbsp(30ml) honey, 1tbsp sesame oil
1/2tsp five spice powder

COOK'S TIPS

Always dip your knife in boiling water, then dry, before cutting into a meringue. It will slice perfectly.

You will get a greater volume of whipped egg white if the egg, the bowl and the beaters are all at room temperature. To make good shaped meringues, add a pinch of baking powder to the egg and sugar mixture.

To store meringues, cool thoroughly, wrap in foil or arrange in an airtight tin with greaseproof paper between each layer. They will keep for up to two months.

Glace fruits in flans with a couple of melted lemon jelly cubes in a little water or with the juice from tinned fruit, thickened with cornflour or arrowroot.

When using banana in a fruit salad, cover the unpeeled banana with cold water for 15 minutes before use. This should prevent it going black in the salad.

Bananas will freeze successfully if you peel and slice them before placing in an airtight container.

Use ginger biscuits instead of sponges at the base of a trifle Cover trifles with a mixture of crushed meringue shells and whipped cream. Grate chocolate on top.

For chantilly cream, whisk a small carton of double cream. In a separate bowl whisk one egg white until stiff. Fold in the cream, one tablespoon of caster sugar and a drop of vanilla essence. Serve chilled.

Increase the volume of double cream by mixing two parts double cream with one part single. Or when half-way through whipping a 1/4pt(150ml) double cream, dilute with 2 tablespoons of milk or plain yoghurt for a lighter effect.

Store cartons of sour and double cream upside down in the refrigerator to keep them fresh longer.

Pipe unused whisked fresh cream into rosettes on a baking sheet and freeze for dessert decoration at a later date.

DESSERTS

CRUNCHY FRUIT CRUMBLE

21/2lb(1kg) cooking apples, peeled, cored and sliced
2oz(50g) castor sugar
1lb(450g) frozen fruits of the forest, thawed
1tsp cornflour
3oz(75g) plain flour
11/2oz(40g) butter
2oz(50g) wholewheat muesli

Oven 350°F/180°C/Gas 4.
Place the apples in a pan with 3-4tbsp water and cook gently, covered for 10 minutes until apples soften. Strain the juice from the fruits of the forest and add to the pan. Mix the cornflour with 1tbsp water and add to the pan. Cook, stirring, for 3 minutes until juices thicken. Cool slightly, stir in thawed fruit. Sift flour into a bowl, rub in butter until mixture resembles breadcrumbs, Stir in muesli. Spoon the fruit filling into a 3pt(1.7ltr) ovenproof dish. Sprinkle the crumble on top. Bake for 40 minutes until topping is golden and crunchy. Serves 6-8

GINGER APPLE FINGERS

6oz(175g) self-raising flour
1/2tsp ground ginger
1tsp baking powder
6oz(175g) soft margarine
5oz(150g) caster sugar
3 eggs
8oz(225g) cooking apples, peeled, cored and chopped
11/2tsp finely chopped stem ginger
3tbsp stem ginger syrup
2 red-skinned apples, cored, sliced, dipped in lemon juice
1oz(25g) icing sugar

Oven 325°F/170°C/Gas 3.
10" x 7"(25 x 16.5cm) greased, base lined. Sift the flour, ground ginger and baking powder into a large bowl. Add the margarine, caster sugar, eggs, cooking apples, stem ginger and 2tbsp of stem ginger syrup. Using an electric whisk, beat all the ingredients together until a dropping consistency is reached. Spread the cake mixture in the prepared tin and level the surface. Arrange the apple slices in rows over the mixture and brush with remaining syrup. Bake for 45 minutes. Leave to cool in the tin. Remove the lining paper. Mix icing sugar with 1tbsp hot water until smooth, spread over the top of the cake. Cut into 16 fingers.

LITTLE APPLE CAKES

8oz(225g) plain flour, pinch salt
1/2tsp bicarbonate of soda, 1tsp cream of tartar
4oz(125g) butter, 4oz(125g) caster sugar, 1 egg
Stewed apple and fresh or frozen blackberries

Oven 375°F/190°C/Gas 5.
12 hole patty tin, greased Sieve flour with salt, soda and cream of tartar, rub in butter, add sugar. Beat egg lightly and mix with flour to a stiff dough. Leave to rest for 30 minutes in the refrigerator. Roll out to 1/4"(5mm) thick, cut out 12 x 3"(7.5cm) rounds and line patty tins. Fill with stewed apple and two or three blackberries. Cover with 2" (5cm) pastry lid, pressing the edges down well. Bake for 20 minutes. Remove immediately from patty tins to wire tray. Serve warm dusted with icing sugar.

APPLE TART

4 large cooking apples
8oz(225g) flaky pastry
2tbsp lemon cheese, mixed spice
2oz(50g) sugar

Oven 425°F/220°C/Gas 7.
Grease an 8"(20cm) enamel or tin plate. Roll out the pastry to 1/4"(5mm) thick. Cut a circle 1/2"(1cm) wider than the plate and leave aside. Re-roll the remaining pastry and cut out a circle the same size as the plate. Leave the pastry to rest. Peel and core the apples, cut each apple into eight pieces, place in a saucepan and cover with hot water. Bring to the boil and simmer for one minute. Remove from the heat and drain in a colander. Leave until cool. Place the smaller piece of pastry on the prepared plate, cover with a layer of lemon curd. Place the cooled apples on top, leave 1/2"(2.5cm) of pastry free around the edge. Shake sugar and spice over the apples. Wet the pastry edge with water or milk and place the other circle of pastry on top. Flake up the edge of the pastry. Make a hole in the centre, decorate with leaf shapes cut from any remaining pastry. Brush the top with milk or beaten egg. Dust with a little sugar. Bake for 15 minutes, reduce the heat to 375°F/190°C/Gas5 and cook for a further 10 minutes. Serve warm with cream.

SPICY APPLE ROLL

8oz(225g) plain flour, 4oz(125g) butter, pinch salt
1 egg and a little water

FILLING

2oz(50g) butter melted
1lb(450g) peeled, cored, sliced cooking apples
2oz(50g) All Bran breakfast cereal
1tsp mixed spice, 3oz(75g) brown sugar, 3oz(75g) sultanas

Oven 425°F/220°C/Gas 7.
Make the pastry. Cover and chill for half an hour, knead lightly
into an oblong and roll out about 15"x10"(38cm x 25cm).
Brush the pastry with some melted butter. Mix the other
ingredients together and spread over the pastry. Roll up like a
Swiss roll and neatly tuck in the ends. Lift onto a greased
baking sheet. Brush with remaining butter. Bake for 15
minutes, lower heat to 375°F/190°C/Gas 5 for a further 20
minutes. Remove from the oven and dust with icing sugar and
a little cinnamon. Serve with cream. Serves 6-8

RHUBARB TART

2lb(1kg) rhubarb, cut into 1"(2.5cm) pieces
9oz(525g) caster sugar
4oz(100g) butter
3 eggs, 2tbsp white wine9oz(250g) plain flour
1tsp baking powder
1/4pt(150ml) soured cream
1tsp ground cinnamon
2oz(50g) ground almonds
icing sugar to dredge

Put the rhubarb into a bowl and sprinkle with 4oz(100g) sugar.
Cover and allow to stand 1-2 hours. Cream the butter with
3oz(75g) of the remaining sugar. Beat one egg and add with the
wine to the creamed mixture. Sift in the flour and baking
powder and mix well. Knead until a smooth dough is formed.
Wrap in greaseproof paper and chill for 30 minutes. Roll out
the dough on a lightly floured board and use to line the bottom
and sides of a well greased, loose bottomed 10" round tin.
Oven 350°F/180°C /Gas 4. Strain the rhubarb, arrange the
pieces in the pastry case. Bake for 30 minutes. Beat the cream,
2 eggs and remaining sugar until creamy. Fold in ground
almonds and cinnamon. Remove the flan from the oven, pour
over the cream mixture. Cook a further 20 minutes until
topping is golden. Ease the flan out of the tin and cool
completely. Dredge with icing sugar. Serves 6-8

DESSERTS

RHUBARB CRUMBLE

10-12 sticks rhubarb, 2tbsp redcurrant jelly
2tbsp honey, soft brown sugar, 4oz(100g) plain flour
2oz(50g) butter, 2oz soft brown sugar

Oven 350°F/180°C/Gas 4. Clean and chop the rhubarb into 1"(2.5cm) pieces. Place in a saucepan with the redcurrant jelly and honey. Cook over a moderate heat until the rhubarb is soft but still holding its shape. Remove from the heat and sweeten to taste with brown sugar. Make the crumble by rubbing the fat into the flour until it resembles breadcrumbs. Add the sugar and mix well. Place the cooked rhubarb in an ovenproof dish, shake the crumble mixture on top, bake for 15 minutes until the topping is golden brown.

PEAR & PEACH FRANGIPANE

2oz(50g) self-raising flour, 3oz plain flour
1oz(25g) ground rice or semolina, grated rind 1 lemon
2oz(50g) soft light brown sugar, 5oz(150g) butter/margarine

FRANGIPANE

4oz(125g) softened butter, 4oz(125g) caster sugar
1 egg, beaten
7oz(200g) ground almonds, 1/2tsp almond essence
1tbsp plain flour
2 peaches, peeled, halved, stoned and sliced
2 pears, peeled, sliced and sprinkled with lemon juice
4tbsp apricot jam

Oven 350°F/180°C/Gas 4.
Lightly oiled 7" x 11"(18cm x 28cm) Swiss roll tin. Sift flours into a large bowl, add ground rice and lemon rind. Rub in butter, add sugar, combine the ingredients to form a dough. (or use a food processor) Press the dough into the tin, chill in refrigerator. Make frangipane - cream sugar and butter in mixer until pale and creamy. Add beaten egg, ground almonds, essence and flour and mix until smooth. Spread this mixture over the chilled base. Arrange pear and peach halves in alternating rows on top of the mixture. Bake for 40-50 minutes until golden and firm to touch. Allow to cool a little. Warm apricot jam and brush over tart. Cut into eight squares. Serve warm or cold. To freeze, wrap each piece in cling film and freeze.

PINEAPPLE PUDDING

14oz(400g) tin chopped pineapple
3 eggs, separated, 6oz(185g) caster sugar
1oz(25g) plain flour, 1oz(25g) butter, 1/2oz(12g) sugar

Oven 325°F/160°C/Gas 3.
11/2pt(800ml) oval ovenproof pie dish. Drain the pineapple pieces. Make up the juice to 1/2pt(300ml) with water. Melt the butter, add flour and cook gently for a few seconds, add juice stirring constantly. Add the sugar and egg yolks, beating well. Stir in the pineapple pieces. Put the mixture into a pie dish. Beat the egg whites until fluffy, slowly add the caster sugar, whisking constantly until the mixture is stiff and glossy. Pile on top of pineapple custard. Sprinkle with a little caster sugar. Bake for 20 minutes until top is crisp. Serves 4-6

* *Add 4oz of sultanas to the mix at the same time as the pineapple*

LATTICED PLUM TARTS

1lb(450g) puff pastry
3 egg yolks, 21/2oz(60g) caster sugar, 3tbsp plain flour
9fl oz(250ml) milk, 1/2tsp vanilla essence, 1tsp icing sugar
2oz(50g) caster sugar
12 Victoria plums, stoned and cut into 8 slices
1 egg yolk mixed with 2tbsp milk to glaze

Make egg custard - whisk the egg yolks with one-third of the caster sugar until pale and thick. Gradually fold in the flour. Bring the milk to the boil with the vanilla essence and remaining sugar. Pour one-third into the egg mixture, stirring. Pour back into the pan and gently bring to the boil until thickened. Put into a clean bowl and dot the surface with a few flakes of butter or dust lightly with icing sugar to prevent a skin forming. Roll out two-thirds of the pastry and cut out six 5"(12.5cm) rounds, place on a greased and slightly wetted baking tray. Chill for 20 minutes. Roll out the remaining pastry into a 10"x 3"(25cm x 8cm) rectangle, chill. Put caster sugar and 4fl oz(125ml) water into a pan, heat until sugar dissolves. Add the plum slices and gently poach for one minute. Drain and reserve. Oven 375°F/190°C/Gas 5. Prick the pastry bases with a fork, divide the pastry cream between the bases, spread evenly with a spoon. Arrange 12 plum slices on top of the cream. Brush the pastry rectangle with glaze, cut into 1/8"(3mm) strips. then halve width-ways. Arrange 4 strips on each tart, then 4 more strips on top diagonally. Trim, chill for 10 minutes. Bake for 20-25 minutes until golden.

DESSERTS

PLUM PUDDING

2lb(900g) ripe plums, 1/4pt(150ml) orange juice
6oz(175g) demerara sugar, 1 cinnamon stick
8oz(225g) `no need to soak' apricots
5 eggs, size 3, separated, 6oz(175g) caster sugar
finely grated rind and juice of 1 lemon
4oz(100g) plain flour, sifted
pinch salt
icing sugar for dusting

Oven 350°F/180°C/Gas 4.
Halve and stone the plums and place in a pan with the orange juice, 1/4pt(150ml) water, sugar and cinnamon stick. Bring to the boil and simmer for 10 minutes. Add the apricots and leave to cool. Remove the cinnamon stick and spoon the fruit mixture into an ovenproof pie dish add half the juice. Reserve the remaining juice. Make the sponge topping by placing the egg yolks in a bowl with the caster sugar and whisking until pale and creamy. Whisk in the lemon juice and rind.Gently fold in the sifted flour and salt with a metal spoon. Whisk the egg whites in a bowl until stiff, fold into the yolk mixture. Pour over the fruit base, bake for 40 minutes until golden brown. Remove from the oven, sprinkle with icing sugar. Serve hot with cream. Serves 4-6

* In season use greengages instead of plums

PLUM & APPLE MERINGUE

1lb(450g) red plums, 3 red-skinned eating apples
oz(50g) soft brown sugar, 1/2tsp ground mixed spice
3fl oz(75ml) white wine

MERINGUE

3 egg whites, 3oz(75g) caster sugar
3oz(75g) demerara sugar

Oven 375°F/190°C/Gas 5.
11/2pt(800ml) oval ovenproof pie dish Halve and stone the plums, quarter, core and slice the apples. Place the apples and plums in a pan, add sugar, wine and spice. Bring to the boil and simmer uncovered for 5 minutes. Cool slightly, spoon into pie dish. To make meringue - whisk the egg whites in a bowl until they form stiff peaks. Gradually whisk in the caster sugar, and all but 2tbsp of the demerara sugar. Spoon or pipe the meringue over the fruit filling, covering it completely. Sprinkle over the remaining sugar. Bake for 5 minutes until the meringue is golden

* In season substitute 3 or 4 pears for the apples

PEAR JALOUSIE

12oz(350g) puff pastry
4 soft pears (or 1 can pear pieces), 2oz(50g) ground almonds
1 egg, separated, 3oz(75g) caster sugar
Juice of half a lemon, 2tbsp raspberry or damson jam

Oven 425°F/220°C/Gas 7.
Roll out the pastry to a 9"x 7"(23cm x 18cm) oblong. Cut in two lengthways. Fold one piece in two, lengthways, and make slashes at 1/4"(5mm) intervals almost to the edge. Set the uncut piece of pastry on a greased and slightly damp baking sheet. Moisten the edges with a little beaten egg white. Beat the egg yolk and sugar until creamy, add the lemon juice and ground almonds. Spread the jam over the pastry, cover with sliced pears and top with the almond mixture. Place the slashed piece of pastry over the filling and press the edges well together, flake up in the usual way. Brush over the top with the remaining egg white, sprinkle lightly with caster sugar and bake for 15 minutes until golden and well risen. Lower the heat to 375°F/190°C/Gas 5 for a further 10 minutes. Serve cold with cream or hot with a pear sauce made by combining the juice of half a lemon and reserved pear juice, thickened with a little blended cornflour.

APRICOT CREAM TART

1oz(25g) butter, 6oz(175g) chocolate digestive biscuits
1tbsp sugar, 1tbsp cornflour, 1/4pt(150ml) milk
1 egg yolk, beaten, 2 drops vanilla essence
1lb 4oz(850g) can apricots, drained
1oz(25g) plain chocolate, melted
8"(20cm) loose bottomed cake tin

Melt the butter and add the crushed biscuits, press into the base of tin, chill. Blend the sugar and cornflour together with enough milk to make a smooth paste. Heat the remaining milk and stir in the cornflour mixture. Cook gently until thickened, remove from the heat. Add a little of the custard to the egg yolk and then pour back into the pan and stir well, cook very gently for 5 minutes until the custard is smooth and thick. Add vanilla essence and leave to cool. Puree two-thirds of the apricots until smooth. Spread over the biscuit base. Pour over cooled custard, chill until set. Decorate with remaining sliced apricots, pipe over melted chocolate. Chill for 1 hour before serving. Serves 4-6

FRUIT CRUMBLE TRIANGLES

12oz(350g) self raising flour, 1tsp baking powder
6oz (175g)butter, cubed, 5oz|(150g) caster sugar
1 egg, beaten, 3fl oz(75ml) milk
1/2tsp vanilla essence, 12oz(350g) raspberries

Oven 400°F/200°C/Gas 6.
11" x 7"(28 x18cm) Swiss roll tin, greased.Sift the flour and
baking powder into a large bowl, rub in the butter until it
resembles breadcrumbs. Stir in the caster sugar, divide the
mixture evenly into two bowls. Beat the egg, milk and vanilla
essence in a jug and gradually beat into one of the bowls.
Spread the cake mixture over the prepared tin. Scatter
raspberries over the cake mixture then shake over the crumble
mixture. Bake for 30-35 minutes. Remove from the oven and
leave to cool completely in the tin. Cut into 16 triangles, dust
with icing sugar before serving.

* *On a country walk collect blackberries for this recipe instead of raspberries*

LUXURY BREAD & BUTTER PUDDING

1 orange
3/4pt(450ml) milk
1/4pt(150ml) cream
6 thick slices white bread
2oz(50g) butter, softened
3tbsp marmalade
2oz(50g) no-soak dried apricots, chopped
2oz(50g) sultanas
2tbsp brandy
1tsp ground cinnamon
3 eggs, beaten
2oz(50g) caster sugar

Use a potato peeler and pare the rind thinly from the orange.
Add the rind to the milk and cream in a saucepan. Heat gently
until almost boiling. Remove from the heat and leave to infuse
for about 20 minutes. Strain and discard the orange rind, leave
the milk to cool. Mix the apricots, sultanas and brandy in a
bowl and leave to soak.
Oven 350°F/180°C/Gas 4. Lightly butter a shallow
21/2pt(1.4ltr) ovenproof dish. Spread each slice of bread with
butter and marmalade. Remove the crusts and cut the slices of
bread into 24 triangles. Scatter the soaked fruit over the base of
the dish. Arrange the triangles of bread on top in rows.
Sprinkle with cinnamon. Whisk the eggs and sugar until pale
and creamy. Slowly add the infused milk to give a smooth
custard mixture. Pour over the bread, pressing down the
triangles to absorb the custard. Leave for 15 minutes. Cook for
1 hour until mixture is set and top is golden. Serve hot with
cream. Serves 6

QUEEN OF PUDDINGS

4oz(100g) fresh white breadcrumbs
1oz(25g) caster sugar, 1tsp finely grated lemon rind
1pt(600ml) milk, 1oz(25g) butter, 3 egg yolks, size 3
3tbsp warmed apricot jam
3 egg whites, 6oz(185g) caster sugar

Put breadcrumbs, sugar and lemon rind into a basin and toss lightly together. Heat the butter and milk in a pan until the butter melts. Pour onto the breadcrumb mixture, stir well and leave for 30 minutes.
Oven 325°F/160°C/Gas 3. Beat egg yolks and stir into the breadcrumb mixture. Put into a 2pt(1ltr) greased, ovenproof dish. Bake for 30 minutes, until firm and set. Remove from the oven and spread with warm jam. Make meringue by whisking egg whites until fluffy, very gradually add the caster sugar, whisking constantly until the meringue is shiny. Cover the jam with swirls of meringue, bake for a further 15-20 minutes until meringue is pale gold. Serve with fresh cream. Serves 6

KIWI SLICES

Oven 375°F/190°C/Gas 5.
Roll out 8oz(225g) puff pastry and line a 4"x 8"(10 x 20cm) oblong tin. Bake blind for 15 minutes. Cool and cover with pastry cream. Arrange slices of kiwi on top. Coat with apricot glaze. Decorate with cream.

PASTRY CREAM

2 eggs, 4oz(125g) caster sugar
2oz(50g) flour, 1/2oz(12g) custard powder
1pt(600ml) milk, vanilla pod or essence

Whisk the egg and sugar in a bowl until white. Mix flour and custard powder. Boil milk, whisk in eggs, sugar and flour, mix well. Return to a clean pan, stir until boiled. Add vanilla essence, remove from heat, pour into a basin. Sprinkle with caster or icing sugar to prevent a skin forming.

* *This works equally well with fresh ripe mangoes*

DESSERTS

APRICOT & ORANGE ROULADE

9oz(250g) pkt ready to eat, dried apricots
finely grated rind and juice of 1 orange
4 medium eggs, separated
3 level tbsp ground almonds
6 level tbsp apricot conserve or jam, icing sugar

Oven 375°F/190°C/Gas 5.
12" x 8"(30x20cm) Swiss roll tin, base lined. Place the apricots and half of the orange rind in a food processor, add the orange juice and puree until smooth. Beat the egg yolks and almonds together until pale in colour, fold into the apricot mixture. Whisk the egg whites until stiff, fold into the apricot mixture. Pour into the tin and bake for 20-25 minutes, or until firm to touch. Remove from the oven and allow to cool in the tin for 5 minutes. Turn onto a sheet of greaseproof paper that has been dredged with icing sugar. Peel away the lining paper, cover with a slightly damp cloth and leave to cool. Mix the apricot conserve or jam with the remaining orange rind and spread over the cooled roulade. Using the greaseproof paper, roll up the roulade lightly. Sift over a little icing sugar and then using a hot skewer, mark a criss-cross pattern on the top. Serves 6

APRICOT TREACLE TART

5oz(125g) wholemeal flour, 4oz wholemeal self-raising flour
5oz soft margarine, 6tbsp fresh breadcrumbs
5tbsp golden syrup, 1tbsp black treacle
finely grated rind 1 lemon, 2tbsp lemon juice
1 can apricot halves in fruit juice, drained

Oven 375°F/190°C/Gas 5.
Make the pastry and chill for 30 minutes. Roll out pastry to line 9" flan tin. Mix together the breadcrumbs, syrup, treacle, lemon rind and juice. Arrange the apricot halves in the pastry case, round side up. Spoon the syrup mixture over them. Bake for 20-25 minutes, cool in tin. Roll out remaining pastry and cut out 6 small, leaf shapes. Bake for 10 minutes until golden. Place around the edge of the tart before serving. Serves 4-6

CITRUS BAKED BANANAS

Put bananas in a greased baking dish with juice 1 orange, juice of half a lemon, grated fresh root ginger, pinch of cinnamon and nutmeg, 1tbsp brown sugar, 1tbsp butter and bake for 15 minutes

* Serve with two dollops of vanilla or coconut ice cream and a paper umbrella!

GINGER CREAM LOG

10oz(275g)pkt ginger nut biscuits, 4tbsp sherry
3/4pt(450ml) cream, whipped stiffly
1oz(25g) stem ginger, drained and chopped into slivers
1oz(25g) chopped walnuts

Dip the biscuits in the sherry and sandwich together with half the whipped cream in a row to form a log. Insert small pieces of stem ginger into the cream. Cover completely with the remaining cream. Sprinkle with chopped walnuts and chill for at least 2 hours until firm.

* As a rich alternative use chilled Marscapone cream instead of whipping cream

COFFEE BRANDY LOG

2tbsp coffee essence, 2tbsp orange juice
3/4pt(450ml) cream, whipped stiffly, 1tbsp brandy
10oz(275g)pkt choc-chip biscuits

Stir the coffee essence into the orange juice. Fold the brandy gently into the whipped cream. Dip each biscuit into coffee mixture and sandwich together in 3 groups of 4 biscuits with half the cream. Arrange the groups of biscuits on a plate to form a log. Cover completely with the remaining cream. Chill for 2 hours. Decorate with chocolate curls.

BAKED BANANAS

3oz(75g) unsalted butter, 3oz(75g) muscovado sugar
2tbsp lime juice, 2tbsp dark rum
1/2tsp star anise, 1/2tsp cinnamon
8 small bananas, 1oz(25g) chopped walnuts

Oven 350°F/180°C/Gas 4.
Beat the sugar and softened butter until pale and creamy, beat in the rum and lime juice. Add the spices. Place the peeled bananas side by side in an ovenproof dish and spread the butter mixture evenly over them. Bake for 10-15 minutes until bubbling. Decorate with a sprinkling of chopped walnuts and serve with fresh cream.

LEMON MOUSSE

1 pkt lemon Jelly, 5tbsp water
2oz(50g) sugar, juice of 2 lemons
4 large egg whites, 1/2pt(300ml) cream

Melt the jelly in water over a low heat, add the sugar and stir
until dissolved. Stir in lemon juice, leave to cool. Whisk egg
whites and add to jelly when it is at setting point. Fold in
whipped cream. Pour into a glass bowl and leave to set.
Decorate with whipped cream. Serves 6-8

STRAWBERRY TART

PASTRY

4oz(100g) plain flour, 1/2tsp mixed spice
2oz(50g) ground almonds
3oz(75g) caster sugar, 3oz(75g) unsalted butter
3 egg yolks. size 3

TOPPING

3oz(75g) mascarpone cheese
5tbsp redcurrant jelly, 1tbsp Cassis or Grand Mariner
1lb strawberries, halved or sliced
1/2pt(300ml) fresh cream

Oven to 375°F/190°C/Gas 5.
Make the pastry - sift the flour and spice into a food processor,
add sugar and butter, process in short bursts until like
breadcrumbs, add almonds, give a short burst, add egg yolks
and process until the mixture is combined. Remove from the
processor, knead lightly, wrap in cling film and chill for 30
minutes. Roll out on a lightly floured surface until 6" in
diameter. Place on a baking tray and roll out to 10" diameter.
Trim the edge neatly and pinch with fingers to give a fluted
edge. Prick all over. Chill a further 30 minutes (pastry can be
frozen at this stage). Bake the pastry for 10-15 minutes until
golden. Leave to cool on tray for one minute before turning
onto a wire rack to cool completely. Transfer onto serving plate,
spread mascarpone cheese over the pastry, arrange the
strawberries on top. Melt the redcurrant jelly with liqueur over
a gentle heat. Spoon liberally over the strawberries to give a
thick even glaze. Leave to set. Decorate with whipped cream,
chill up to two hours. Serves 4-6

STRAWBERRY TRIFLE

8oz(225g) strawberries, 1oz(25g) plain chocolate
2oz(50g) trifle sponges
2tbsp strawberry jam, 4tbsp white wine
2tbsp custard powder
1oz caster sugar, 1/2pt(300ml) milk
1/4pt(125ml) cream
8oz(225g) strained Greek yoghurt

Hull all but 4 of the strawberries. Break the chocolate into pieces and melt in a bowl over a pan of hot water. Halve the 4 reserved strawberries and dip the narrow end in the melted chocolate. Leave to set. Halve the trifle sponges, sandwich together with the jam and cut into small squares. Put in the base of a 2pt(1.2ltr) glass bowl with the hulled strawberries. Sprinkle the wine over. Mix the custard powder, sugar and 4tbsp milk to form a thick paste. Bring the remaining milk to the boil and gradually stir into the custard mixture. Return to the pan and stir over a low heat until thick. Cover the surface with wetted greaseproof paper and leave to cool. Spoon the custard over the sponge and fruit. Whip the cream until soft and fold in the yoghurt. Spoon over the custard, swirl gently with a fork. Arrange the chocolate dipped strawberry halves on top before serving. Serves 4-6

CHUNKY STRAWBERRY CHEESECAKE

1lb(450g) strawberries, juice 2 oranges
2oz(50g) caster sugar
8oz(225g) digestive biscuits
1oz(25g) caster sugar, 4oz(100g) melted butter
1pkt strawberry jelly
1/4pt(150ml) water
8oz(225g) cottage cheese, 5oz(125g) cream cheese

Roughly chop the strawberries and put into a bowl with the orange juice and caster sugar. Leave aside while preparing the base. Finely crush the digestive biscuits and mix with caster sugar and melted butter. Spread over the base of a lightly greased spring-clip 9"(23cm) tin, pressing down well. Refrigerate for 20 minutes. Dissolve the jelly in the water and allow to cool. Put the cottage cheese, cream cheese, juice strained from prepared strawberries and cooled jelly. Buzz for a few seconds. Stir in the chopped strawberries and pour the mixture into the prepared base. Chill for at least one hour before serving. Decorate with whipped cream and whole strawberries. Serves 6

Marbled Raspberry Mousse

4oz(100g) caster sugar, 4 eggs, 2oz(50g) plain flour
icing sugar for dusting
2tsp gelatine, 1/2 pkt raspberry jelly
12oz(325g) raspberries, 1/2tsp vanilla essence
1/4pt(125ml) cream, 8oz(225g) strained Greek yoghurt

Oven 350°F/180°C/Gas 4.
2lb(900g) loaf tin lined with cling film. Whisk together
2oz(50g) caster sugar and two eggs in a bowl until thick and
creamy. Sift the flour and gently fold into the mousse mixture.
Pour into a greased and lined 10" x 7"(26cm x 18cm) Swiss roll
tin. Cook for 8-10 minutes until well risen and pale golden.
Place a sheet of greaseproof paper on top of a tea towel and dust
with icing sugar. Turn the sponge out onto the paper. Stir
gelatine into 2tbsp warm water, leave to soak for five minutes,
dissolve over a pan of hot water or in the microwave for 30
seconds. Melt raspberry jelly in 3tbsp hot water. Reserve 12
raspberries, push the remainder through a sieve, stir in the
melted jelly to the puree, cool until thick. Whisk the
remaining 2oz(50g) caster sugar, 2 eggs and vanilla essence
until thick and creamy. whip cream until it forms soft peaks.
Fold into the vanilla mixture with the yoghurt and the melted
gelatine. Add the raspberry puree, swirl together to give a
marbled effect, spoon into prepared tin. Trim the sponge to fit
the top of the tin, press onto the mousse mixture. Chill for at
least 4 hours until set. Turn onto a serving plate and remove
cling film. Decorate with reserved raspberries. Serves 6

Poached Pears in Mulled Wine

5oz(150g) granulated sugar, 1/4pt red wine
rind and juice 1/2 lemon
4 whole cloves, 1"(2.5cm) cinnamon stick
4 large ripe pears
1tsp arrowroot or cornflour
cream to serve

Put the sugar, wine, 1/4pt(150ml) water, cinnamon, cloves,
lemon and rind into a pan and heat gently until the sugar has
dissolved. Bring to the boil and boil for 2 minutes. Peel the
pears, cut in half and remove the cores with a spoon. Add to the
spiced wine and simmer for 20 minutes or until pears are
tender. Turn frequently during cooking. using a slotted spoon,
transfer the pears to a serving bowl. Boil the syrup until
reduced by half. Mix the arrowroot with the lemon juice, add to
the syrup, stirring until thickened. Strain over the pears, cover
and chill for at least four hours. Serve with shortbread biscuits.

* *Alternatively use 4 large cooking apples instead of pears*

SHORTBREAD BISCUITS

7oz(200g) butter, 3oz(75g) icing sugar
8oz(225g) plain flour

Oven 275°F/140°C/Gas 2.
Cream the butter and icing sugar together. Add flour, mix together. Roll out on an 8"(20cm) round metal tray. Put into a greased baking tray and bake for 15 minutes. Cool on wire tray.

* Add 11/2tsp of mixed spice to the baking mix

LEMON CHEESECAKE

11/2oz(40g) butter, 2 level tbsp golden syrup
6oz(125g) digestive biscuits
3tsp gelatine (or 1pkt lemon jelly) dissolved in juice 1 lemon
8oz(225g) cottage cheese, sieved
2oz(50g) icing sugar, 1/4pt(150ml) cream, whipped
2 egg whites, whisked firm
A lightly greased, spring-clip 9"(23cm) tin

Make base by crushing biscuits and mixing with melted butter and syrup. Combine the cottage cheese, icing sugar and cream. Fold in egg whites, add dissolved gelatine or jelly. Smooth over base and chill for at least 1 hour. Decorate with whipped cream and chocolate. Serves 6

BAILEY'S CHEESECAKE

6oz(175g) shortbread biscuits, crushed
2oz(50g) ground almonds
3oz(75g) melted butter, 8oz(225g) cream cheese
2oz(50g) caster sugar
1 egg, separated
1/4pt(150ml) fresh cream
4 shots of Bailey's Cream Liqueur
2tsp gelatine

Combine the biscuits and almonds with melted butter. Grease and line base of 9" tin, press the biscuit base into the tin and chill. Beat cream cheese, sugar and egg yolk until smooth. Lightly whip the cream and fold in. Stir in the Bailey's into the mixture until well combined. Sprinkle gelatine over 4tbsp water, leave to soak, then dissolve over a pan of simmering water. Allow to cool, stir into the cheesecake mixture. Whisk the egg white (soft peaks), fold into the mixture. Pour into the tin and chill for 2-3 hours. Serves 6

DESSERTS

NICE CHEESECAKE

7oz(200g) butter, softened, 4oz(100g) caster sugar
7oz(200g) cream cheese, 1 egg, size 3, 1tsp lemon juice
1/2tsp cinnamon, 6tbsp brandy, 6tbsp milk
30 Nice biscuits

SAUCE

4tbsp caster sugar, 4tbsp water, 2tbsp cocoa, 4oz chocolate
1oz(25g) butter, whipped cream, chocolate flake bar

Cream the butter and sugar until light and fluffy. Add cream cheese, egg, lemon juice and cinnamon and mix well. Mix brandy and milk together in a basin. Lay out a large piece of foil on a flat surface. Dip the biscuits in the brandy and milk, lay them on the foil in 3 rows x 5 biscuits lengthways in each row. Spread a thin layer of the cheese mixture over the biscuits and cover with the remaining biscuits dipped in brandy and milk. Spread the rest of the cheese mixture down the centre row of biscuits. Pull up the foil sides gently to make the cake into a triangular shape. Refrigerate overnight. Boil the sugar, water, cocoa and chocolate in a saucepan for 2 minutes. Remove from the heat, beat in butter, cool. Remove the foil and place the cake on a serving dish. Brush the melted chocolate over the cake and allow to set. Decorate with whipped cream and crumbled flake. Serves 6-8

FLAKY FRUIT PIE

8oz(225g) cottage cheese
1tbsp cornflour, 1oz(25g) caster sugar
1tsp grated lemon rind, 1lb(450g) mixed soft fruits
6 sheets filo pastry, 1oz flaked almonds, icing sugar

Oven 400°F/200°C/Gas 6.
Sieve cottage cheese into a bowl. Stir in cornflour, sugar and grated lemon rind. Mix well. Hull fruits, slice strawberries. Lay 4 sheets filo pastry in a 7"(18cm) greased flan dish, allowing ends to overlap slightly. Spoon half the fruit onto the pastry. Spread over the cheese mixture then cover with remaining fruit. Fold pastry edges up over the filling. Scrunch up rest of pastry and put on top of pie to completely cover filling. Sprinkle pie with almonds and cook for 5-6 minutes. Dust with icing sugar.

CHOCOLATE CREAM SAUCE

6oz(150g) dark chocolate, 1oz(25g) butter, 4tbsp double cream.

Melt the chocolate and butter in a bowl over a pan of simmering water. Cool slightly and stir in double cream.

BRANDY SNAPS

2oz(50g) butter
2oz(50g) granulated sugar
2oz(50g) golden syrup
2oz(50g) plain flour, 1tsp ground ginger
1/4pt(150ml) cream, whipped

Oven 325°F/160°C/Gas 3.
Place butter, sugar and syrup in a pan over a low heat and stir until melted. Sift together the flour and ginger, stir into the melted mixture. Grease a large, shallow baking tray and place 4 teaspoonfuls of the mixture well apart on it. Bake for 8 minutes until golden. Remove the tray from the oven and leave for one minute before lifting off with a palette knife. Quickly wrap around the handle of a wooden spoon, slide off gently when firm, leave on a wire tray until cold. Repeat with remaining mixture. Fill ends with whipped cream. Makes 16.

PROFITEROLES

1 quantity of Choux pastry (see pastry chapter)
1/2pt(300ml) cream, whipped
3tbsp icing sugar

Oven 425°F/220°C/Gas 7.
Grease a large shallow baking tray and run the cold tap over it, shake off any surplus water. Pipe or spoon 20 equal amounts of choux pastry, well apart, on the prepared tray and bake for 25 minutes, until golden and well puffed. Remove from the oven and make a small slit in each bun, return to the oven for a further 5 minutes. Cool on a wire rack. An hour before serving, fill with whipped cream and dust with icing sugar. Serve with luke warm chocolate cream sauce. Choux buns can be open frozen when cooked and then packed into rigid containers for up to 3 months. When required, thaw and crisp in a hot oven for 2 minutes.

CHOCOLATE SAUCE

3oz(75g) caster sugar, 3oz(75g) soft brown sugar
3oz(75g) cocoa powder, 1/2pt(300ml) milk
1tsp vanilla essence, 1oz(25g) butter

Put all the ingredients into a saucepan over a low heat and stir until dissolved. Slowly bring to the boil stirring, then cook briskly, without stirring for 2 minutes or until the sauce coats the back of a spoon.

VANILLA PUFFS

1 quantity of Choux Pastry

FILLING

2 eggs, lightly beaten, 2oz(50g) caster sugar, 2tbsp flour
2tbsp cornflour, 1/2pt(300ml) milk, few drops vanilla essence
1/4pt(150ml) double cream, 2oz(50g) icing sugar

Oven 400°F/200°C/Gas6.
Spoon or pipe six balls of choux pastry onto the greased and
wetted baking sheet. Bake for 20-25 minutes, remove from the
oven, make a slit in each, return to the oven for a further 5
minutes. Cool on a wire rack. Make the filling - Beat the eggs
and sugar together until pale and creamy. Sift in the flour and
cornflour, beat into the mixture with a little milk, until
smooth. Pour the remaining milk into a saucepan and heat
until almost boiling. Pour onto the egg mixture, stirring well.
Return to the saucepan and heat gently, stirring, until thick.
Add vanilla essence and cook a further 2 minutes. Remove from
the heat, pour into a bowl, cover tightly with greaseproof paper
and leave until cold. Whip the cream until it holds soft peaks,
fold into the cold custard. Split each puff in half and fill with
the custard, cover with top half. Dust with a little icing sugar.
Sift the remaining icing sugar into a bowl, add 1-2tsp water.
Mix well until mixture coats the back of a spoon. Drizzle the
icing over the top of each bun. Serve chilled.

CHOCOLATE MOUSSE

1/4pt(150ml) sugar syrup
4oz(125g) sugar, 4oz(125g) water}
7oz(200g) Bournville chocolate
1/2pt(300ml) cream, lightly whipped
Jamaican Rum, 2 egg whites

Make the sugar syrup - place the sugar and water in a pan over
a medium heat, stir until the sugar crystals have dissolved, then
let it come to the boil, and boil for exactly three minutes.
Remove from the heat and stir the syrup into the melted
chocolate. Fold in the cream then the whisked egg whites. Add
rum. Place in a glass bowl and allow to set. Decorate with
cream. Serves 4-6

CHOCOLATE MARQUISE

7oz(175g)plain dark chocolate
31/2oz(90g) unsalted butter, 3oz caster sugar
2tbsp cocoa, 1/2tsp instant coffee powder
3 egg yolks, 2tbsp rum, 1/2pt(300ml) cream, lightly whipped
4oz(100g) sponge fingers, flake bar, cream for decorating

Melt chocolate in a bowl over a pan of hot water. Beat the softened butter with half the sugar until pale and creamy. Beat in cocoa and coffee. In a clean bowl whisk egg yolks with the remaining sugar until creamy. Whisk in rum. Beat the slightly cooled, melted chocolate into the cocoa mixture, fold in the egg mixture and the whipped cream. Line a deep 6"(15cm) souffle dish with cling film, spread a little of the chocolate mixture on the sides of the sponge fingers and arrange, with sugar side out, around the dish. Spoon in the remaining mixture to the dish. Chill for at least 4 hours until firm. Trim the sponge finger to the same height as the filling. Shortly before serving turn out onto a plate and decorate the top with rosettes of whipped cream and sprinkle with crumbled flake. Serves 6-8. Freeze in individual portions.

MOCHA MERINGUE

3 egg whites, size 3, 6oz(175g) caster sugar
8oz(225g) plain chocolate
2tbsp coffee essence, 2tbsp maple syrup
5tbsp Greek yoghurt, 6oz(175g) mascarpone cheese
2oz(50g) plain chocolate

Oven 250°F/130°C/Gas
1/2. Line a baking sheet with parchment paper and mark two 5" x 10" (12.5cm x 25cm) oblongs on the parchment. In a clean bowl whisk the egg whites until stiff, whisk in the caster sugar, 1tbsp at the time to make a firm glossy meringue. Spoon into a piping bag fitted with a large star nozzle. Pipe zigzag lines to fill the marked areas. Bake for 1 hour until crisp, cool on a wire rack. Place the chocolate, coffee essence and syrup in a bowl over a pan of hot water. Heat gently until mixture is melted and smooth. Remove from the heat, leave to cool and thicken slightly. In a separate bowl, fold the yoghurt into the mascarpone cheese. then gently fold into the cooled chocolate mixture. Just before serving, sandwich the two meringues with the chocolate mixture. Drizzle some melted chocolate over the top and serve. Serves 4-6

COOK'S TIPS

For a special occasion, use slices of Battenburg cake instead of ordinary sponge finger in a trifle.

Make a quick sweet sauce topping by cutting up a bar of fudge and melting it with one tablespoon of hot water. Add some chopped nuts and glace cherries. Serve with ice-cream and desserts.

For a tasty dessert, place peach halves cut side uppermost, on a grill pan. Top each peach with halved marshmallows and heat under a medium grill until the marshmallow melts and turns golden brown.

To clean strawberries, soak for a short time in water with one teaspoonful of vinegar added. This will remove all small insects. Rinse well.

To enhance the flavour of strawberries, cover with orange juice and leave stand for 30 minutes before serving. Orange flavoured liqueurs could also be added.

Cook pears in lemonade instead of water to keep them white and taste sweeter.

To keep fruit whole when stewing, always bring the water or syrup to the boil before adding the fruit, then simmer gently.

When making rhubarb pie or crumble, add a slice of banana and mixed spice before cooking.

For baked apples - remove the core stuff the centre with mixed dried fruit. Stand the apples in a shallow dish, sprinkle with brown sugar. Put a knob of butter on top and bake until tender. Instead of the sugar use honey or treacle

Make apple crisps, peel and core apples, cut into thin slices, place on an oiled baking tray and cook at 375oF/190oC/Gas 5 until crisp.

If a custard or sauce starts to go lumpy as it's cooking, plunge the base of the pan into a basin of cold water and whisk until smooth again.

Whole seedless grapes set in a lime jelly and topped with cream makes a refreshing sweet.

CHOCOLATE BISCUIT ICE CREAM

1 can evaporated milk, well chilled
6oz(185g) soft light brown sugar
3/4pt(450ml) fresh cream
10oz(275g) chocolate digestive biscuits

Pour the cold evaporated milk into a mixing bowl and whisk until thick and creamy. Gradually whisk in the sugar. Whisk the cream until it forms soft peaks, fold into the milk mixture. Crush the biscuits and fold in. Put the mixture into a rigid container, cover and freeze (there is no need to stir during freezing). Remove from the freezer and allow to stand at room temperature for 15-20 minutes before serving. Serves 6-8

Ice's & Sorbets

Basic Ice Cream

31/2fl oz(100ml) water, 21/2(65g)sugar
3 egg yolks, 3/4pt(450ml) cream

Make the sugar syrup by melting the sugar in water then boil rapidly without stirring until syrup reaches 215-220oF or short thread. Beat the egg yolks to a mousse, gradually add the sugar syrup, beating well. Add flavouring - vanilla, coffee, chocolate, fruit etc. Whip cream, fold into egg mousse. Put into a freezer-proof container and freeze until firm. Serves 6-8

Fruity Ice Cream

4oz(100g) granulated sugar, 1/4pt(150ml) water
4 egg yolks
1pt(600ml) cream, 1tsp vanilla essence
1lb(450g) luxury dried fruit mix, 1/4pt(150ml) port

Soak the fruit in port overnight. Dissolve the sugar and water in a saucepan over a gentle heat. Then boil briskly for 3 minutes until it forms a syrup. Whisk the egg yolks until creamy, slowly add the sugar syrup, whisking continuously until the mixture is thick and mousse like. Whip the cream, fold into the egg mousse with the vanilla essence. Stir in the fruit. Pour into a bowl and freeze for 2 hours, remove from the freezer and stir gently to distribute the fruit. Return to the freezer and leave until frozen.

Double Chocolate Bombe

4oz(100g) plain chocolate, broken into pieces
1tbsp brandy
2tbsp coffee essence, 1tbsp cocoa
2 eggs, size 3, separated
1/2pt(300ml) cream, lightly whipped
8oz(225g) white chocolate, broken into pieces
4tbsp milk, 1/2pt(300ml) cream, lightly whipped

Place the plain chocolate, brandy, coffee essence and cocoa powder in a heatproof bowl over a pan of hot water. Heat until melted and mixture is smooth. Remove from the heat and cool for 5 minutes. Whisk the egg yolks and stir into the chocolate mixture. In a clean bowl, whisk the egg whites until stiff. Gently fold in the whipped cream into the mixture and then gently fold in the whisked egg whites. Pour into a 2pt(1.2ltr) pudding basin, place a smaller basin inside and push down until the mixture comes up evenly around the sides to the top. Freeze for 4-5 hours or overnight. Melt the white chocolate with the milk over a pan of hot water. Cool for 10 minutes, fold in the whipped cream. Remove the ice cream from the freezer, twist out the inner bowl and pour the white cream mixture into the centre. Cover and return to the freezer for 5 hours. Leave at room temperature for 10 minutes before serving. 6-8

Vanilla Chocolate Bombe

VANILLA ICE CREAM

7oz(200g) caster sugar
8 egg yolks
1pt(600ml) single cream
1 vanilla pod, 1/2pt(300ml) double cream

CHOCOLATE MOUSSE

6oz(185g) dark chocolate, 3tbsp strong black coffee
4 eggs, separated
1/2oz(15g) butter, softened
1tbsp brandy, 3tbsp caster sugar
1/4pt(150ml) double cream, whipped

Make the ice cream by placing the sugar and egg yolks in a bowl and whisking until thick and creamy. Put single cream and the vanilla pod in a heavy based saucepan an simmer for 3 minutes. Cool slightly, then remove the vanilla pod. Gradually add half of the warm cream mixture to the egg mixture, beating well, then add the egg mixture to the remaining cream. Stir over a low heat until the mixture thickens and coats the back of a spoon. Do not boil. Set aside to cool. Stir in the double cream and pour into a freezer-proof bowl lined with cling film. Freeze until almost set. Remove from the freezer, break up with a fork and put into a food processor. Process until thick and creamy. Pour into a 3pt(1.8ltr) bowl lined with cling film. Cover a 1pt(600ml) bowl with cling film and press down into the mixture, forcing the ice cream up around the sides. Freeze until firm. To make the chocolate mousse, break the chocolate into small pieces and place it and the coffee in a bowl, melt over a saucepan of simmering water, stirring until smooth. Remove from the heat, beat in egg yolks one at the time. Continue beating, add butter and brandy, allow the mixture to cool. Beat the egg whites until soft peaks form, then beat in the sugar. Fold egg whites and cream into the chocolate mixture. Remove smaller mould from the ice cream, spoon the mousse into the centre of the ice cream and return to the freezer to set. Serves 6-8

Raspberry Parfait

1lb(450g) raspberries
6fl oz(200ml) cream, 4oz(120g) cream cheese
8oz(250g) icing sugar

Wash the raspberries and liquidise into a purée. Push through a nylon sieve to remove seeds. Whisk the cream cheese and icing sugar together in a mixer, add the raspberry purée and mix well. Whip the cream until stiff and stir into the mixture. Place the mixture in a ring tin, 2lb(900g) loaf tin or small ramekins, lined with clingfilm. Freeze overnight. Remove from the freezer, just before serving with fresh raspberries. Serves 6-8.

* Other soft fruits such as strawberries, apricots, black or red currants could also be used. Increase the sugar for more acid fruits such as black or red currants.

BAKED ALASKA

2 egg whites, 4oz(50g) caster sugar
4 small sponge bases, ice cream, strawberries or raspberries

Oven 450°F/230°C/Gas 8.
Make the meringue - put the egg whites in a clean dry bowl and beat until stiff and peaky. Gradually add the caster sugar and whisk until the mixture is stiff and glossy. Place sponge bases on a tray well apart. Put a layer of fruit on the base and top with a large scoop of ice cream. Cover the ice cream totally with the meringue and place on the top shelf of a hot oven for 2-3 minutes until the meringue begins to brown. Serve immediately. For a large Baked Alaska use a flan case as the base.

BLACKCURRANT SORBET MERINGUE LAYER

1lb(450g) fresh or frozen blackcurrants, 2tbsps water
4 egg whites, 8oz(225g) caster sugar
1tsp white wine vinegar, 1tsp cornflour

Oven 140°C/275°F/Gas 1.
Cook the blackcurrants in water until the fruit softens, cool. Draw two circles 7"(18cm) diameter on baking parchment, and place on a baking sheet. Whisk egg whites until very stiff, gradually whisk in the sugar. Fold in the vinegar and cornflour. Reserve half the meringue, divide the other half between the two circles of parchment and spread out evenly, but not quite to the edge. Bake for 2 hours. Sieve the blackcurrants into the reserved meringue. Fold together, freeze for 3-4 hours, stir half way through. Place one meringue in the base of a loose bottomed 8"(20cm) cake tin, cover with half the sorbet, repeat, cover with clingfilm, return to the freezer until frozen. Decorate and serve immediately. Serves 4-6

ORANGE SORBET

1/2pt(300ml) water, 6oz(175g)sugar
1/2pt(300ml)fresh orange juice
juice 11/2 lemons
2 egg whites

Combine the water and sugar in a saucepan, bring to the boil and boil over a high heat for five minutes. Leave to cool. Combine the syrup and fruit juice and pour into a shallow freezing tray. Freeze until mixture has crystallised, but not completely solid. Whisk the egg whites until stiff. Break up the partially frozen ice and put into a food processor. Process until smooth. Add the egg whites and process until these are incorporated. Return to the freezing tray and freeze until solid.

ASTRY

FLAKY PASTRY

1lb(450g) plain flour, 1tsp salt
8oz(225g) margarine, 4oz(125g) Cookeen, frozen
1tsp lemon juice, 1/2pt(300ml) water

Chop frozen fats into a bowl. Add sifted flour and salt. Mix together and combine with water and lemon juice. Put onto a floured board and roll out into a rectangular shape. Fold up the bottom third of the rectangle and fold the remaining third over it. Roll out to the original size. Repeat the folding and rolling procedure four times. Cut into two pieces and place each piece in a freezer bag and freeze until required. When required, defrost in the refrigerator, roll out into a rectangle shape and repeat folding and rolling 2-3 times more before using.

SHORTCRUST PASTRY

8oz(225g) plain flour, pinch salt
6oz(175g) very cold butter, 1 egg

Oven 350°F/180°C/Gas4. Whizz the flour and cubed butter in a food processor until it resembles rough breadcrumbs. Whisk the egg, use three-quarters of it to bind the mixture in a bowl. Do this by hand or with a metal knife. Wrap the dough in cling film and cool for at least 30 minutes. Roll out the dough and rest for a further 20-30 minutes.

SWEET PASTRY

8oz(225g) plain flour, pinch salt
1/2tsp baking powder, 1tsp cream of tartar
4oz(125g) butter, 4oz(125g) caster sugar, 1 egg

Sieve flour with salt, soda and cream of tartar, rub in butter, add the sugar. Beat egg lightly and mix flour to a stiff dough. Leave to rest for at least 30 minutes in the refrigerator. Roll out to 1/4"(5mm) thick.

CHOUX PASTRY

21/2oz(75g) plain flour, pinch salt, 1/4pt(150ml) water
2oz(50g) butter, 2 eggs, size 3, well beaten

Sift flour and salt twice. Put water and butter into a saucepan over a low heat until butter is melted, bring to a rolling boil. Lower heat and add all the flour. Stir briskly until the mixture forms a soft ball and leaves the sides of the pan clean. Put the mixture into a food mixer, while beating at medium speed, gradually add egg until the mixture is smooth and shiny, it should stand in soft peaks. Use immediately or cover tightly to prevent the pastry drying out.

COOK'S TIPS

Using butter as the fat will give the pastry a better flavour.
Since coolness and minimal handling are the key points for
shortcrust, use a food processor to cut up cold hard fat into the
flour quickly.

Do not add too much liquid as this will make the pastry tough
and shrink on baking.

The finished dough should just cling together and not feel
damp to touch. Resting the pastry dough is very important.
Wrap the dough in cling film and refrigerate for at least 30
minutes before using. Freezing of pastry can be done at this
stage.

To ensure crisp pastry, always use a metal baking tin.
If pastry is to have a wet filling it is essential to pre-bake the
base. You can either bake blind, lined with greaseproof paper
and weighed down with dried peas or freeze the lined tart tin
and bake directly from frozen.

Another method to avoid a soggy pastry base is to brush the
partially baked crust with egg white or egg wash and bake to
set the egg.

AKES

CHOCOLATE CAKE

8oz(225g) plain flour
8oz(225g) caster sugar, 1tsp baking powder
11/2oz(40g) cocoa
1/2pt(300ml) milk, 1tbsp vinegar
2 eggs, 1tsp vanilla essence
4oz(100g) melted butter

ICING

1lb(450g) icing sugar, 1 egg, 2oz(50g) soft butter
2tbsp cream, 11/2oz(40g) cocoa, 1tsp vanilla essence

Oven 350°F/180°C/Gas4
Two 8"(20cm) greased sandwich tins. Sieve the dry ingredients together into a bowl. Beat the two eggs, add milk, vinegar, essence and melted butter. Stir the liquid into the dry ingredients and mix well, do not beat. Divide the mixture evenly between the sandwich tins. Bake for 25-30 minutes. Cool in tins for a few minutes before turning out onto a wire rack. To make icing - beat the egg and soft butter, add the sieved icing sugar and cream. Add sieved cocoa and vanilla essence and beat well. Use icing as filling and covering for cake. This cake will keep in a sealed tin in a cool place for up to two weeks

MADEIRA CAKE

8oz(225g) plain flour sieved with 11/2tsp baking powder
6oz(175g) soft margarine, 6oz(175g) castor sugar, 3 eggs

Oven 325°F/160°C/Gas 3.
Use a 7" deep cake tin, base lined and greased. Place all the ingredients in a mixing bowl and beat until well mixed. Place in tin. Smooth top and put a strip of citron peel on top. Bake for 11/2 hours.

COFFEE CAKE

8oz(225g) self-raising flour
8oz(225g) caster sugar, 8oz(225g) soft margarine
4 eggs, size 3, 2tbsp coffee essence

Oven 350°F/180°C/Gas4
Two 8"(20cm) greased sandwich tins. Cream the margarine and sugar, add beaten eggs with a little flour and beat well. Stir in coffee essence. Fold in sieved flour. Divide the mixture between two sandwich tins. Bake for 25-30 minutes. Cool in tins for a few minutes before turning out onto a wire rack. Make icing as for chocolate cake - use 2-3tbsp coffee essence instead of the cocoa.

SPONGE CAKE

4 eggs, size 3, 4oz(125g) caster sugar
4oz(125g) self raising flour

Oven 350°F/180°C/Gas 4.
2 x 8"(20cm) round sandwich tins, greased. Whisk the eggs and sugar in a mixer until thick and creamy. Gently fold in the sieved flour. Pour into the prepared tin and bake for 10 minutes until light brown. Cool on a wire rack.

GLAZED LEMON SQUARES

8oz(250g) self-raising flour, 11/2tsp baking powder
6oz(175g) caster sugar, 6oz(175g) soft margarine
3 eggs, size 3, grated rind 2 lemons, 3-4tbsp milk
juice 2 lemons, 4oz(125g) granulated sugar

Oven 350°F/180°C/Gas 4.
7"x11"(18x28cm) shallow cake tin, greased. Sift the flour and baking powder, add the sugar, margarine, eggs, lemon rind and milk. Using a wooden spoon or beater, mix well, then beat the ingredients together until smooth. Spoon the mixture into the prepared tin and spread level. Bake for 40 minutes until firm to touch. Heat the lemon juice and sugar until it dissolves. When the cake is cooked, remove from the oven and spoon the warm glaze over the top. Leave until cold. Serve cut in squares with a little sugar sprinkled on top.

CARROT & ORANGE CAKE

4oz(125g) butter, 1tbsp grated orange rind
4oz(125g) castor sugar, 2 eggs, size 3
8oz(225g) sultanas, 10oz(275g) grated carrot
8oz(225g) self-raising flour
1tsp nutmeg, mixed spice, 1tbsp orange juice

FROSTING

2oz(50g) butter, 8oz(225g) icing sugar
1tbsp orange juice, orange food colouring

Oven 300°F/150°C/Gas 2
2lb loaf tin, base lined and greased. Cream butter, rind and sugar. Beat in eggs one at the time. Add sultanas, carrot, dry ingredients and orange juice. Spread in tin. Bake for 11/2hours. Leave in tin 5 minutes before turning out onto a wire tray. Make frosting - cream the butter until light and fluffy. Gradually add icing sugar, orange juice and a few drops of colouring. Beat until spreadable.

GINGER MARMALADE CAKE

3oz(75g) butter, 3oz(75g) light soft brown sugar
4tbsp black treacle, 4tbsp marmalade
6oz(185g) plain flour, 1tsp ground ginger
1/2tsp bicarbonate soda
4fl oz(90ml) milk, 1 egg beaten

ICING

2-3tsp lemon juice, 2oz(50g) icing sugar
3 pieces stem ginger, 3oz mixed red and green glace cherries

Oven 325°F/160°C/Gas 3.
Greased and lined 2pt(1.2ltr) ring-mould tin Stand ring on a baking sheet. Place butter, treacle, marmalade and sugar in a small pan and heat gently, stirring, until mixture is melted and smooth. Cool. Sift the flour, ground ginger and bicarbonate soda into a bowl. Pour in the melted mixture, egg and milk and beat until smooth. Pour into prepared tin and bake for 25-30 minutes. Leave to cool in the tin for five minutes before turning out onto a wire rack. To decorate, stir in lemon juice to sifted icing sugar and beat until smooth. Drizzle over the ring cake, scatter chopped ginger and glacé cherries.

FRUIT TWIST

1lb(450g) self-raising flour, 1tsp salt
4oz(125g) margarine, 2oz(50g) caster sugar
2oz(50g) sultanas, 2oz(50g) mixed peel
2oz(50g) glace cherries, chopped
2 eggs, size 3, grated rind of 1 lemon, 8tbsp milk
ICING

3oz(75g) icing sugar, lemon juice
1oz(25g) chopped glacé cherries, 1oz(25g) mixed peel

Oven 350°F/180°C/Gas 4.
2pt ring tin, base lined and greased. Sift dry ingredients and rub in margarine. Add sugar, sultanas, mixed peel, and cherries. Beat eggs and lemon rind together and add to flour mixture with enough milk to make a soft, but firm dough. Divide the dough in half and knead each piece lightly. Shape each piece into a 20"(50cm) roll. Twist the two rolls together, place in greased ring tin. Bake for 25 -30 minutes. Make icing - blend the icing sugar with enough lemon juice to give a thick coating consistency. Spoon icing over the hot cake. Mix the cherries and mixed peel. Sprinkle over icing

BOILED FRUIT CAKE

1lb(450g) mixed fruit, 6oz(175g) butter, 12oz(350g) sugar
1tsp mixed spice, 1tsp bread soda
1 x 432g tin crushed pineapple
12oz(350g) self-raising flour, pinch salt
3 eggs, size 3

Oven 325°F/160°C/Gas 3.
8"(20cm) round cake tin, greased, base lined. Put the first five ingredients into a saucepan, stir in the pineapple. Bring to the boil over a medium heat and simmer for 3 minutes. Cool in the pan. Sift the flour and salt, add to the mixture. Beat the eggs lightly and add. Mix thoroughly. Pour into the prepared tin and bake for 11/2 - 2hrs.

STICKY TEA BRACK

8oz(225g) margarine, 10oz(275g) sugar
2lb(900g) mixed fruit
4oz(125g) cherries, 2oz(50g) mixed peel
4oz(125g) chopped dates, 4oz(125g) dried apricots
2oz(50g) walnuts
1/2pt(300ml) cold strong tea, dash brandy or whiskey
2tsp breadsoda

Oven 350°F/180°C/Gas 4
2 x 2lb(900g) loaf tins, well greased. Put all the above ingredients into a saucepan and bring to the boil. Simmer for 15 minutes. Cool, then add :-

12oz(350g) plain flour, 2tsp baking powder,
1/2tsp ginger, mixed spice, nutmeg
4 eggs, beaten

Combine the ingredients and bake for 1 - 11/2 hours. If the top of cakes are browning too quickly, cover with cardboard. Do not remove from the tin until cool.

APPLE ROCK CAKES

8oz(250g) plain flour, 2tsp baking powder, 1tsp cinnamon
4oz(125g) butter or margarine, 1 cooking apple (about 8oz)
3oz(75g) caster sugar, 4oz(125g) sultanas
2 eggs, size 3, 1oz(25g) icing sugar

Oven 375°F/190°C/Gas 5.
2 flat baking sheets, greased. Sift the flour, baking powder and cinnamon together. Rub in butter or margarine. Peel, core and chop the apple, stir into the dish with the sugar and sultanas. Beat the eggs and use to combine the mixture. Put rough spoonfuls of the mixture onto the baking sheets. Bake for 20-25 minutes. Sprinkle with a little icing sugar.

COOK'S TIPS

When making sweet pastry, work in a little vanilla essence into the margarine before rubbing in the flour.

Use milk instead of water when mixing icing sugar, it gives a lighter texture, has a creamier taste and reduces the sweetness.

When mixing icing for butterfly cakes, put in two teaspoonfuls of your favourite jam for instant flavour and colour.

To soften brown sugar, place in a bowl and cover with a damp cloth for an hour.

Use cold coffee instead of milk when making spiced fruit cake or gingerbread, it gives a delicious flavour.

When making fruit cakes or scones, soak the dried fruit overnight in pure juice for a lovely flavour.

Add a tablespoon of marmalade with fruit when making fruit scones, it keeps them moist.

If dried fruit becomes hard, put it in a colander over a pan of hot water and leave for a few minutes to plump up.

To stop the top of a cake cracking, lightly brush with water before baking.

When making a treacle tart, grate a ginger biscuit on top.

Use a potato peeler to make thin strips of orange or lemon peel. Freeze for use in baking.

When baking fat-free cakes such as a Swiss roll sponge, dust the tin with flour instead of greasing or it will stick.

Before filling a sponge with jam or cream, spread a thin layer of soft butter or margarine on the base. This will prevent the filling soaking into the sponge.

If a sponge cake collapses in the middle, cut out the centre to make a flan ring instead and fill with fruit and fresh cream.

After baking, rub the inside of the mixing bowl with flour to pick up all remaining sticky dough. The bowl is now easy to wash.

READ

POTATO BREAD OR FADGE

6oz(175g) potatoes mashed with butter and a little milk
4oz(125g) plain flour
salt and pepper

Combine the potatoes and seasoned flour. Knead lightly on a floured board and roll out a quarter of an inch thick. Cut into rounds or triangles. Bake on floured, preheated griddle or pan until well skinned on both sides. Serve hot with butter or reheat by frying in fat.

* *Grate 4oz of cheddar cheese into the mixtur*

WHEATEN BREAD

1lb(450g) plain flour, 14oz(400g) wholemeal
1/2 cupful each of coarse bran and wheatgerm
2tbsp sugar, 1tsp salt, 4 level tsp bread soda
2 eggs, buttermilk (about 1 litre)

Oven 450°F/230°C/Gas 8.
Sift all the dry ingredients well together. Add eggs beaten with some buttermilk. Add more buttermilk until the mixture is a soft consistency. Grease a roasting tin (or two 2lb loaf tins) and shake a little flour over the base. Put the mixture into the baking tin (or tins) and lightly level with a spoon. Shake some wholemeal over the top and make a few marks with a knife. Bake for 30-35 minutes. Remove from tin onto a wire tray to cool. This bread freezes very well.

AFTERNOON TEA SCONES

12oz(350g) plain flour, pinch salt
2oz(50g) margarine
11/2tsp bread soda, 11/2tsp cream of tartar
1tbsp sugar
2oz(50g) sultanas
1 egg, buttermilk

Oven 450°F/230°C/Gas 8.
Sift dry ingredients into a bowl. Rub in margarine. Add sultanas. Beat egg with a little buttermilk and combine with dry ingredients. Mix to a soft but workable dough. Roll out on a floured board and cut with a 3"(7.5cm) cutter into 12 rounds. Place on a greased tray and bake in hot oven for 20 minutes. Cool on a wire tray.

SCOTCH PANCAKES

8oz(225g) plain flour, 1tsp bread soda
1oz(25g) sugar pinch salt, 1 egg
1/2pt(300ml)buttermilk

Preheat heavy pan or griddle. Put all the ingredients into a mixer bowl and beat until mixture is a thick dropping consistency - add more buttermilk if required. Grease or oil pan and drop tablespoonfuls into rounds - do not overlap. Turn over when bubbles appear on the top and the bottom is golden. Cook other side till golden. Cool on wire tray or in a clean teatowel. Serve warm or cold with butter, honey or jam. Makes approx 12 pancakes.

SINGIN' HINNY OR WELSH CAKES

12oz(350g) self-raising flour
2oz(50g) ground rice
2oz(50g) sugar, 1tsp salt
1oz(25g) butter/margarine
1oz(25g) Cookeen
3oz(75g) currants
1 egg, size 3
1/4pt(150ml) milk (approx)

Preheat griddle to moderate heat and grease well. Mix together dry ingredients. Rub in the fats, add currants. Mix to a soft, but manageable dough with egg and milk. Roll out into a large circle - 1/4"(5mm) thick. Cut into equal- sized triangles and cook scones for 3-4 minutes on each side. Serve hot.

TREACLE SCONES

1lb(450g) plain flour, pinch salt
2tsp cinnamon, 2tsp mixed spice
2tsp bread soda
11/2oz(40g) caster sugar
2oz(50g) butter
2tbsp black treacle
1/4pt(150ml) strong black tea

Oven 450°F/230°C/Gas 8.
Sift the dry ingredients, add sugar and rub in butter. Rub a spoon with oil or use a hot spoon to measure the treacle. Add to the dry ingredients with tea and a little milk if required. Turn onto a floured board and knead lightly. Flatten out to 1/2"(1cm) thick and cut into 12-15 rounds. Bake for 15 minutes. Cool on wire tray.

SODA FARLS OR GRIDDLE SCONES

10oz(275g) plain flour, 1tsp bread soda
1oz(25g) sugar
Buttermilk, pinch salt

Preheat griddle or heavy frying pan. Sieve and sift all the dry ingredients. Add enough buttermilk to make a soft, but manageable dough. Divide into four and roll each piece lightly in flour. Shake a little flour onto the griddle and place the four scones on it. Turn over after 7 minutes or when the top of the scone feels warm. Cook a further 7 minutes. Cool on a wire tray. These are best eaten the day they are made, served with butter and jam.

PLAIN MUFFINS

8oz(225g) plain flour
4oz(125g) brown sugar, 4oz(125g) margarine
6oz(175g) desiccated coconut
2tsp baking powder, 1/2tsp salt, 1/2tsp mixed spice
4oz(125g) mixed dried fruit
2 eggs, milk

Oven 400°F/200°C/Gas 6.
12 hole muffin tin, lined with paper cases (or base lined with circles of greaseproof paper). Sieve flour, salt, spice and baking powder in a bowl. Rub in margarine. Add remaining dry ingredients. Beat eggs and add to mixture. Add milk if necessary - mixture should be of a dropping consistency. Half fill the prepared muffin tins with the mixture. Bake for 5 minutes then reduce temperature to 350oF/180oC/Gas 4 for further 15-20 minutes until golden.

JAM & COCONUT MUFFINS

10oz(275g) plain flour, 1 egg, size 3
2tsp bread soda (or 3tsp baking powder)
1/2pt(300ml) buttermilk or milk
4oz(125g) caster sugar
6tbsp vegetable oil
4oz(125g) coconut, 3tbsp jam

Oven 400°F/200°C/Gas 6.
Grease a 12 hole muffin tin. Sift flour and raising agent into a large bowl. Stir in sugar and coconut. Beat the egg, milk and oil together, stir into flour mixture. Place a large tbsp. of mixture into each muffin tin. Put a teaspoon jam in the centre and then spoon more mixture on top until the tin is two-thirds full. Bake for 25-30 minutes until well risen and firm to touch.

RAISIN BRAN MUFFINS

3oz(75g) wholemeal flour, 3oz(75g) plain flour
11/2tsp bread soda, pinch salt
1tsp ground cinnamon, pinch mixed spice
1oz(25g) bran, 2oz(50g) raisins
1 chopped cooking apple
2oz(50g) brown sugar, 2oz(50g) granulated sugar
1 egg
8fl oz(240ml) buttermilk or yoghurt
juice half a lemon, 2oz(50g) margarine melted

Oven 400°F/200°C/Gas 6.
Grease and line nine deep muffin tins or a twelve bun tin. Sift together flours, bread soda, salt, spices. Stir in bran, raisins and sugar and chopped or grated apple. Mix together the egg, buttermilk, lemon juice and melted fat. Stir into dry ingredients. Do not beat mixture. Divide evenly between patty tins. Bake for 20 minutes until well risen. Serve warm or cool. Freeze for up to 3 months

GARLIC BREAD

1 French loaf or Vienna Roll, 4oz(100g) butter
2 cloves garlic, crushed, salt and pepper

Cut the loaf into thick slices but not through the bottom crust. Combine the butter and garlic and beat until soft. Season well. Spread the garlic butter over each slice, keep a little for the top. Wrap the whole loaf in foil and seal the edges well. Bake in a moderate oven for 10 minutes until crisp on the outside and hot and soft inside.

BON APPETIT!

NDEX

INDEX

NDEX